+ AUB Human

First published in Great Britain in 2020
by AUB Human

Arts University Bournemouth
Wallisdown, Poole, Dorset BH12 5HH

ISBN 978-1-8382310-0-2

Edited by Alice Stevens
Designed by Natalie Carr
Printed and bound in Great Britain by Dayfold

FSC
www.fsc.org
MIX
Paper from
responsible sources
FSC® C018381

aub.ac.uk/aub-human

+ AUB Human

Published by

AUB Human

AUB HUMAN

AUB Human is a platform that celebrates social, ethical and sustainable creative practice and aims to inspire others to think and practice responsibly. It connects designers, architects and other creative practitioners, both on campus and beyond, who share a desire to bring about positive change for global good.

At the heart of AUB Human is critical debate. Debate takes many forms; conference, exhibition, workshops and through project work, all of which challenge our creative community to address the most pressing issues our world currently faces. Whether it be an environmental problem, inequality or a global pandemic, the desire is to use our creative skills, in whatever capacity we can, as a force for good, in order that we can play our part in helping to create a more inclusive and sustainable planet.

Alice Stevens
AUB Human Founder

AUB Human started as an embryo of an idea a few years ago. Under the watchful eye of Alice Stevens, it has grown to become pervasive across AUB as a uniting philosophy. AUB is deeply committed to educating the next generation of creatives and designers who will be prepared to address some of the major societal issues and global challenges of humankind, with all the compassion and humility we can muster.

AUB courses are changing their curricula, experimenting and innovating with delivery methods whilst understanding and contributing to the critical contexts in which work is made. Staff and students as co-creators are our secret super power in taking on these challenges with AUB Human at its heart.

Professor Emma Hunt
Deputy Vice Chancellor

FOREWORD

Professor Paul Gough
Vice-Chancellor, Arts University Bournemouth
October 2020

Throughout 2020, while developing the 2030 Strategy for Arts University Bournemouth (AUB), the ethos of AUB Human was at the heart of our combined endeavour. Working at pace and with a sense of urgency that reflected the environmental and societal challenges all around us, we created an engagement process that sought contributions from all parts of the university, including the Student's Union, alumni and our external stakeholders.

Through a programme of workshops, task and finish groups, informal conversations, and open feedback loops, we tuned into the historic achievements of the university and interrogated its essential personality, but we also looked adventurously and ambitiously towards the horizon to see how we could shape new futures.

During the development of the Strategy, AUB Human was one of our touchstones: it has long proved to be a living example of a cross-disciplinary and polyvocal gathering of staff, students, alumni and external contributors who have long brought ideas and provocations into the campus.

But it was clear to me that AUB Human was not only a community of thinkers and makers. Its raison d'etre and its conceptual base was grounded in remaining relevant. Taking such frameworks as the United Nations Sustainable Development Goals, the group gather regularly to share projects and programmes of creative work designed around core values that bring fresh energy to local and global concerns.

A refreshed set of values is at the centre of our new Strategy: 'Passion', the fourth of these values, encapsulates all that AUB Human stands for:

'Education transforms lives: a creative education transforms society. Through our sense of purpose and determination for the best education, research and partnering with industry, we empower our people to learn, grow and connect. We care about the work we do, the respect we have for each other, and the powerful sense of belonging that characterises everything we do.'

We also committed to promoting greater inclusivity and wider involvement, to reaching out because we know we are better for our diversity.

Over the past five years AUB Human has proved that we are enriched by the depth of respect we have for each other and the strength of our relationships with our people, our places and the planet.

Our revised framework of values aligns with everything that AUB Human has aimed for and achieved. Through dialogue and discussion, through projects and praxis, AUB Human has remained attuned to the imminent opportunities and to the real challenges of the Anthropocene, reminding us what it is to inherit the values of a humanistic education and to remain committed to working with those who are different to us, or challenge us, so that we can grow stronger together, creating new synergies, global connections and sustainable futures.

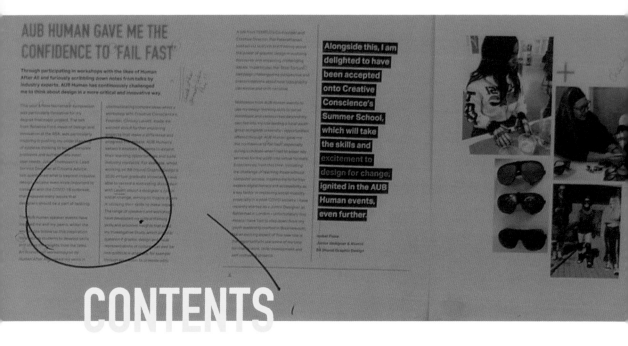

CONTENTS

CONTENTS

DAYS
FOR GIRLS

In March, AUB Costume and
Performance Design Department ran
an epic day of making in support of
the Days for Girls charity, a non-profit
organisation dedicated to creating
a free, dignified, and educated
world through providing access
to sustainable feminine hygiene
solutions and health education.

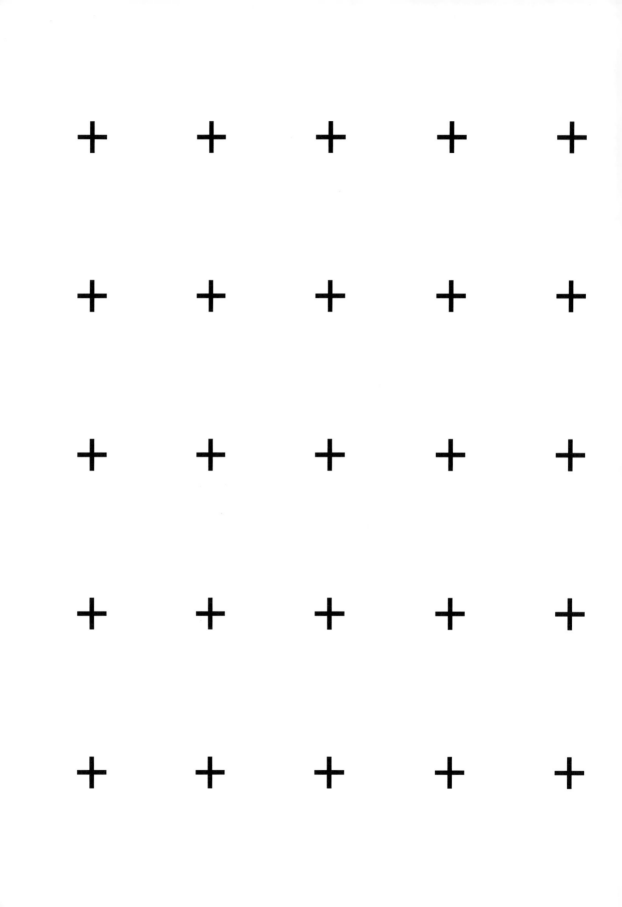

INTRODUCTION

This year I have been the first AUB Human Graduate Intern.

This book, a personal project and collaboration between Alice Stevens and myself, has been created during the Covid-19 pandemic whilst the university campus was closed. The book celebrates some of the AUB Human events, projects and symposia I have been fortunate enough to be a part of during the 2019-2020 academic year.

Whilst a student at Arts University Bournemouth, AUB Human challenged me to think more deeply about what creativity can achieve and introduced me to an alternative approach to design; shaping my focus as well as my career goals. In my work as a designer, I have chosen to tackle issues of ethics, sustainability and social problems, exploring how design can offer solutions in helping to create a better and fairer world for all.

I hope you enjoy exploring some of the projects we have organised this year, and hearing from AUB students, staff and the many inspiring speakers who have generously shared their time and insights with us.

Natalie Carr
AUB Human Graduate Intern

New Narratives

Symposium
March 2020

The New Narratives symposium challenged
current practices and proposed new ways
of thinking, doing and making in order to
help achieve an inclusive, sustainable and
regenerative world.

We were delighted to be joined by industry
professionals and academics to debate this
critical topic.

Convenor: Alice Stevens
Co-convenor: Karen Ryan and Monica Franchin

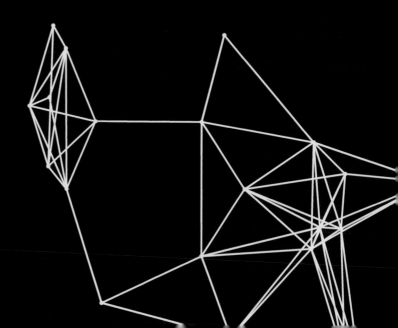

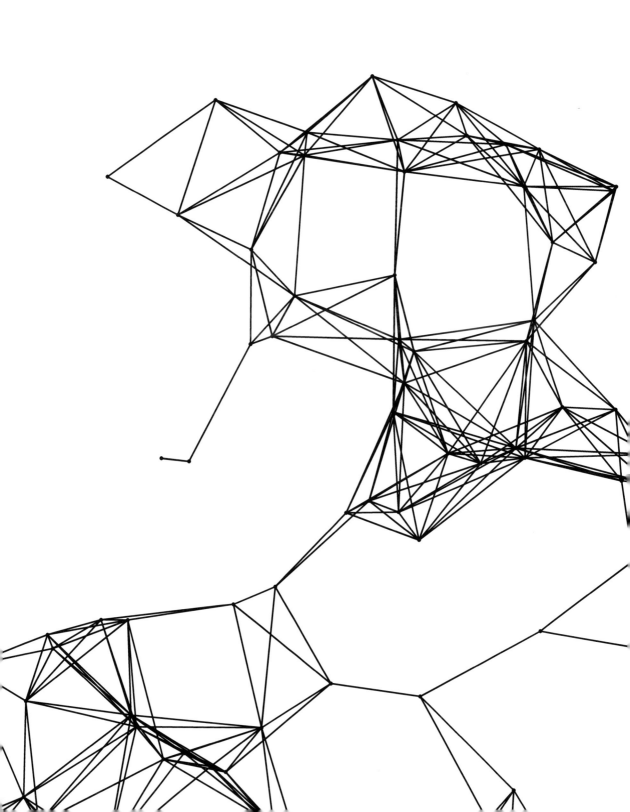

New
Narratives

SPEAKERS

Ruth Andrade is originally from Brazil and grew up in a concrete jungle, amidst high-rise buildings, asphalt and pollution, witnessing first-hand the destruction of the natural environment, which prompted an early interest in environmental issues. She started working for Lush in 2004 and became the head of environment. Ruth has three key aims: lead brand strategy on regenerative impact, support organisational development based on living systems and help evolve our charitable giving strategies. She is passionate about transforming business into a force for regeneration and leveraging the power of a global brand to do good.

Mark Chivers is a life-long activist and has been actively campaigning on climate change for over a decade. A qualified engineer, he has worked in financial services for much of his career alongside training as a presenter with the Climate Reality Project and studying for a BSc in Geography and Environmental Science. He co-founded and is now leading the Zero Carbon Dorset project, which aims to identify what Dorset needs to do to be a net zero county by 2030.

Rob Nicoll is a material lead designer with a strong focus on developing novel solutions to growing global problems. He graduated with a degree in Design from Kingston University with accompanying awards in Product Innovation and Material Development. Using his design background, Rob is responsible for showing brands how bio-materials can be utilised without compromising on quality or aesthetic, with a focus on fast-moving industries, including fashion and interior architecture.

Dr Sue Thomas is currently Assistant Professor of Fashion at Heriot-Watt University. She wrote and now teaches the pioneering new MSc Ethics in Fashion for the School of Textiles and Design. Having taught in the UK and New Zealand, it was in Australia that she began teaching fashion design for sustainability. An active public speaker and broadcaster (Tedx Talk in 2016), she is an advocate for ethics, sustainability and inclusion. Her book Fashion Ethics was published by Routledge in September 2017.

Rebecca Ford is Head of Design & Innovation at social change charity the RSA, where she brings together human-centred design, systems thinking and innovation methods to accelerate the RSA's mission: uniting people and ideas to resolve the societal challenges of our time. Rebecca has spent the past decade managing the strategic development and delivery of social innovation programmes.

Julian Thompson is a Designer and Strategist committed to making significant progress on social challenges and enabling organisations to have meaningful impact for those they serve. With over 10 years experience in the public and third sectors, Julian uses his interdisciplinary background in community organising, innovation, strategy and policy to design services and solutions which balance the needs of people, communities and organisations. His design practice is centred on inclusion, equity and systems thinking.

Ram Shergill captures a kaleidoscope of different cultures through his photography. Merging bio-integrated design with adornment, his work explores metamorphosis, taking on the concept of Deleuze and Guattari's theories of 'becoming other'. His work has been exhibited worldwide, showing at Somerset House, the V&A and Whitechapel Gallery amongst others. Ram Shergill's work is in the permanent collection at The National Portrait Gallery. Ram continues to contribute to international editions of Vogue, Harper's Bazaar, and many other publications. Ram's PhD research is situated at UCL The Bartlett School of Architecture, in which he is combining methods of photographic exploration with bio-integrated design, employing new narratives in design practice as a radical and critical response to climate change, anthropocentrism, and speciesism.

How can the planet be better because humans exist?

Ruth Andrade
**Regenerative Impact,
Earth Care & Giving, Lush**

Life is constantly renewing its capacity to generate more life. But the question is how can we create an economy that actually follows these principles? Rather than an economy that is degenerative and actually creates death.

How can we align our human economy to the economy of the rest of nature? Remembering that we are also nature.

How can we align human systems to the same natural systems that created us?

No system can sustain itself over the long term if it's not designed to continuously regenerate.

How can we designers really take on this challenge, to create and design for a system that can continuously regenerate?

MARK CHIVERS

The Climate Reality Project & Co-founder, Zero Carbon Dorset

Global warming and climate change have been reported in the news for decades. Numerous declarations, commitments and initiatives have been launched and, in late 2015, the whole world came together to sign up to the Paris Agreement, an achievement almost unique in human history.

Yet, behind the agreements, behind the declarations, the collective inaction of our governments has seen the risk of the impacts of climate change escalate from a crisis into a full-blown emergency. Scientists tell us our emissions need to drop dramatically this decade to avoid the worst consequences of catastrophic, irreversible climate breakdown and ecological devastation.

Mark Chivers asked, 'Must we change, can we change, will we change?' in a presentation that outlined the scientific evidence and real-life impact of the climate crisis, detailed the encouraging growth in renewable energy and other exciting solutions to the problems, and provided a sobering conclusion that, while we have the answers, the actions required, in the time available, have yet to materialise.

At its heart, the climate emergency is a human emergency – one that threatens our health, well-being, economy and potentially our very existence. It is already having an impact on those communities least capable of protecting themselves or recovering. Many of today's refugees have already been displaced by climate change. Yet, the solutions are not only viable but also beneficial, particularly to those marginalised communities, and could create a cleaner, safer, more equitable world.

Act, like your world depends on it. Because, your world depends on it!

How can we see ourselves as part of the systems we're trying to change?

REBECCA FORD

Head of Design & Innovation, RSA

At the RSA we believe in a world where everyone is able to participate in creating a better future. This year has brought into sharp relief some of the major challenges we face in doing that, from climate change and global health crises to continued racial injustice and structural inequality. These problems are systemic: they are complex and interconnected, unpredictable and constantly changing, and there's no easy answers or single fix.

Combining systems thinking with design, 'systemic design' is an emerging practice that can help us unravel and address the challenges of our time. It pushes us to think more deeply, more long term, and about the bigger picture when it comes to these messy problems. And it helps us to navigate where and how we design interventions in the here and now.

These are some of the questions we're carrying with us in the RSA Design & Innovation team and we invite you to explore too:

As designers, how can we submerge ourselves deeper into problems we're living through? How can we engage different perspectives and design collaboratively with them? How can we see ourselves as part of the systems we're trying to change and be willing to change ourselves?

Find out more:

RSA's Living Change Approach:
thersa.org/approachRSA

RSA Student Design Awards:
thersa.org/student-design-awards

With the challenges we are facing in the world increasing in complexity, interconnectedness and uncertainty, how might designers adapt and respond?

Rebecca Ford
Head of Design and Innovation
The RSA

JULIAN THOMPSON

Service Design Lead, Citizens Advice
& Founder, Rooted By Design

Designers are arguably in more powerful positions than ever, from working on Government policy to designing critical public services and addressing climate change. With this power comes the responsibility to design inclusively, ensuring the impact of our solutions reach as many people and communities as possible.

Is inclusive design practice enough to create more equal and just futures for us all?

+

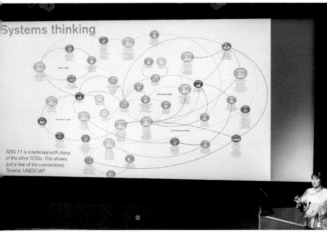

Systems thinking

SDG 11 is interlinked with many of the other SDGs. This shows just a few of the connections.
Source: UNESCAP

Leave the world Lusher than we found it. 🌍

DR SUE THOMAS

Assistant Professor of Fashion, Heriot-Watt University

> **It was the best of times, it was the worst of times, it was the age of wisdom, it was the age of foolishness, it was the epoch of belief, it was the epoch of incredulity, it was the season of Light, it was the season of Darkness, it was the spring of hope, it was the winter of despair...**

—Charles Dickens, A Tale of Two Cities

A few weeks after the New Narratives symposium, Covid-19 struck. Two months after that, #BlackLivesMatter. And still, the climate emergency.

It is clear the fashion industry is in a serious state of flux. But this is an opportunity, a potential paradigm shift, to help steer into a new future. The Covid-19 pandemic has proven beyond doubt that the lifecycle of a garment (or any designed object) is not only about the designer, marketer, and customer experience. Suffering is happening in South Asia, where the cancelling of orders (and lack of payment) has meant the workers were unemployed with no other means of support.

Audit your favourite labels – are they paying? Audit your job applications – do you want to work for them?

This is not a single culture, two genders, one colour, one faith problem. The climate emergency is global, thus the solutions need to be inclusive and collaborative. Designers are needed, maybe more than ever: remember it's NOT about you...
It's about US

How might we use bio-materials, without compromising on quality or aesthetic, within fast-moving industries such as fashion and interior architecture?

ROB NICOLL

Co-Founder & CMO Chip[s] Board Ltd

As designers we have to come to terms with the idea that our products will not have long term relevance, with changes in trends forcing redesigns and new challenges.

However, the speed of change in this industry, whilst often seen as wasteful, can be utilised for good. Designers must use these gaps between trends as an opportunity to not just look at aesthetics but to strip each development down to its individual components and rebuild it to improve function for not only the consumer, but society as a whole.

Designers in all industries have now entered the age of consideration. Historically the main considerations for a product were its function and form, but newly widespread principles of 'end of life' and 'circular economy' are now key to modern design processes. These principles are forcing us all to consider the materials that a product is made from, as well as the journey of its components once it has served its purpose.

Although material options have previously been limited, we have entered a time where choice of material can be as endless as your choice of colour. This current expansion in the material market makes for an extremely interesting era to be entering (and disrupting) the design industry.

Newly widespread principles of 'end of life' and 'circular economy' are now key to modern design processes

How can we create better lives using bio-integrated design methods?

Ram Shergill
Artist/Photographer, Editor in Chief

Photo: Porcupine (Ram Shergill)

WEAPONS OF REASON: ICONOTHON WORKSHOP

The Weapons of Reason Iconothon was run by Paul Willoughby and Andrea Dell'Anna from Human After All, a London design agency powered by reason and empathy.

'Weapons of Reason is a publishing project by Human After All (HAA) to understand and articulate the global challenges shaping our world. In a world saturated by photography, image-making has an extraordinary power to better communicate stories that matter. HAA are experts in translating complex ideas into a clear, clean visual language.' (Human After All, 2020)

Issues of Weapons of Reason have been produced in partnership with organisations that share the same values and a desire to inspire change, such as IDEO, Age UK and Greenpeace.

Creating icons with HAA was a really exciting and insightful experience as it pushed me to design icons for complex issues whilst having the challenge of communicating the concept visually

Carl Doneza
Student

In the Iconothon Workshop, students from BA (Hons) Illustration and BA (Hons) Graphic Design created bespoke sets of icons to help communicate important global topics like conflict, misinformation and fake news.

Carl Doneza, a second-year Graphic Design student told us about the workshop. He said, 'Creating icons with HAA was a really exciting and insightful experience as it allowed me to design icons for complex issues such as misinformation, whilst having the challenge of communicating the concept effectively. I have even applied the learning to my most recent project about sustainability. Overall, the AUB Human events this year have been really inspiring and showed me how I can create work that helps society and the planet.'

AUB Human events and the Iconothon have been really inspiring and helped me realise that through design we can change the world for the better

**Martin Nachev
Student**

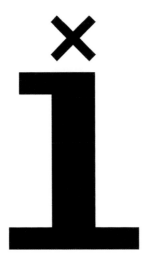

Michael Rozen
Miscommunication

Dan Trend
Miscommunication

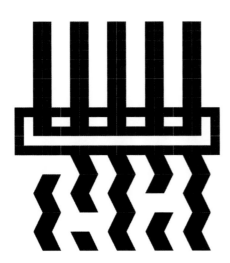

Carl Doneza
Misinformation

Martin Nachev
Misinformation

DAYS
FOR GIRLS

In March, the AUB Costume and Performance Design Department ran a day of making, in support of the Days for Girls charity, a non-profit organisation dedicated to creating a free, dignified, and educated world through providing access to sustainable feminine hygiene solutions and health education.

The event raised funds and awareness to support the creation of washable hygiene kits for girls and women in The Gambia, Africa. Over 250 students and staff worked together to make over 200 kits, using the courses' state-of-the-art equipment in the university costume studios.

The Days for Girls project was principally facilitated by Senior Lecturer Adele Keeley, ably assisted by members of the course team, as well as students from every year level of the course. Level 6 students Maisie Thomas, Eliza Reed and Katy Perks helped supervise the event. They were also joined by Sandra Sherwood, a permanent member of the Days for Girls team, who helped lead the event.

I really like that you're not just making a pack and don't know where it's going to go, we actually saw and met these girls and it was already improving their attendance

Maisie Thomas
Student

It is hoped that working with Days for Girls will enable our students to contribute in helping to solve the problem of period poverty, and to keep girls in schools in countries where basic sanitary products are not available.

Since 2008, Days for Girls has reached over 300,000 women and girls in over 100 countries. Hygiene solutions are a simple and effective way to enable girls to go to school and women to go to work without interruption each month. Student Organisers Maisie Thomas and Eliza Reed visited The Gambia along with tutor Adele Keeley and other volunteers from the Days for Girls programme for 11 days. The team took part in the education programme set up by the Days for Girls charity while in The Gambia. Here, they successfully distributed 1,070 sanitary hygiene packs to pupils from various schools, educating them on how to use the equipment, the importance of basic hygiene and female biology.

The initiative is part of our commitment to raising awareness of socio-political issues and sustainable practice within the student body

**Rebecca Pride
Course Leader**

It was a really nice day of everyone collaborating together. People came into university knowing that they were going to **make a difference** to somebody

Eliza Reed
Student

EMPATHY BUILDING FOR DESIGNERS

Every year, AUB Human runs an empathy building workshop to help students design for people whose lived experience is not of their own. Students have the opportunity to try out various tools and techniques that they can use in their own work to help build empathy and gain greater insight from potential users in order to design or co-create more relevant and innovative solutions.

The workshop was organised by Alice Stevens and run by staff from BA (Hons) Graphic Design, but open to all students on campus.

The first activity students undertake is run by senior lecturer Marten Sims. He tells us, 'The first principle of empathy is being a good listener so for this activity we use an empathy tool called Twenty One Toys. It is actually a puzzle that students must do blindfolded, but to solve the puzzle they must communicate effectively.'

Empathy enables deeper understanding and an ability to see problems from another's perspective which is critical to inclusive and successful design

**Alice Stevens
AUB Human**

+

The tools enabled me to literally 'walk in my user's shoes' — I would never have experienced this if it wasn't for taking part in the workshop

Mia Cann
Student

38

Senior lecturer Mark Osborne who started his teaching career at Hereward College, a specialist residential college for students with disabilities, spoke about the importance of the workshop and added, 'In the workshop activity debriefs, students show an increased level of insight after experiencing the ageing simulation suit and using the wheelchair, highlighting the numerous barriers encountered, both physical and emotional'.

In addition, students also tested simulation gloves designed by Cambridge University and goggles produced by Alzheimer's Research UK that simulate issues a person with dementia might experience. In addition, students tested a tremor simulator and range of glasses that simulate eye conditions such as tunnel vision and diabetic eye.

Mia Cann, 2nd year Graphic Design student, said: 'The empathy workshop really helped me to consider my user's needs. In turn, it also pushed me to prototype my ideas more quickly in order to get insights from my user. The tools enabled me to literally 'walk in my user's shoes'—I would never have experienced this if it wasn't for taking part in the workshop. The main factor I took away from the session was the importance of designing with empathy and to consider human diversity'.

Students show an increased level of insight after experiencing the ageing simulation suit and using the wheelchair, highlighting the numerous barriers encountered, both physical and emotional

**Mark Osborne
Senior Lecturer**

As a museum, we always enjoy supporting AUB Human. MoDiP supports teaching, learning, and research across AUB and beyond.

This year, we looked at the theme of New Narratives through sustainable design in plastics by exploring **what makes a product sustainable,** how it can be used to adapt and change the use of other things, and how easily plastic objects can be regenerated through recycling or upcycling.

Louise Dennis
Museum of Design in Plastics

MODIP

New Narratives in Plastics

2nd – 20th March 2020
Library first floor cases

A pop-up exhibition in response to the AUB Human theme of New Narratives. This exhibition looked at the sustainability, adaptability, and the regenerative uses of plastics in design and was supported by online content on MoDiP's website and blog.

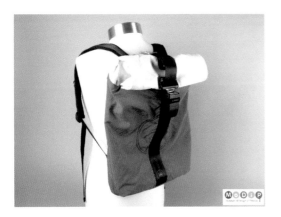

Airpaq backpack, designed by Michael Widmann and Adrian Goosses, 2018. (Museum of Design in Plastics, AIBDC : 008171)

Being Me: Plastics and the body

20th March 2020 – 4th March 2021
Museum of Design in Plastics

Being Me explores the ways in which plastics help us to be ourselves; by changing our shape, keeping us safe, aiding us when our bodies struggle, and keeping us alive. On display are prosthetics, protective clothing and medical equipment.

Pacemaker model, made by AUB modelmaking student Kate Evans 2020, based on the 1958 device invented by Drs Rune Elmqvist and Ake Senning. (Museum of Design in Plastics, AIBDC : 008433)

INTERNATIONAL WOMEN'S DAY 2020

AUB Human marked International Women's Day in March 2020. Taking the campaign theme of #EachforEqual, where an equal world is an enabled world, we were delighted to welcome back three alumni from BA (Hons) Graphic Design to share their journeys and industry experiences since graduating. Introducing the alumni and chairing the panel discussion was AUB Human founder, Alice Stevens.

At AUB our Equality and Diversity Plan describes how we aim to advance our moral, social and legal obligations to put equalities at the heart of every area of activity. The plan is intended to ensure that every member of the University's community is treated fairly and respectfully regardless of the characteristics that may define their identity. It seeks to do more than simply 'promote' equalities and is focused on outcomes and real progress.

63% of graphic design students are women; yet only 17% are Creative Directors

(Kerning The Gap, 2020)

It is important we run events such as these to celebrate the achievements of our talented and creative alumni and learn from their experiences. It is our collective responsibility to challenge stereotypes, fight bias and help create an inclusive and gender equal world.

Alice Stevens
AUB Human

Rosie Isbell

ALUMNI PANEL

Rosie Isbell graduated from BA (Hons) Graphic Design at AUB in 2009. She is a multi-disciplined Design Director specialising in the development of brand-led experiences, services and products. She has collaborated with some of the world's biggest organisations to shape the amazing moments that bring brands to life, applying her natural creative core to complex social, business and cultural challenges. She has worked for studios such as Wolff Olins (London and San Francisco), R/GA, ustwo and frog (Munich), and for clients including Google, Visa, BMW, Disney, Orange, Nokia, Tandem Bank and Hive.

Izzi Hays graduated from BA (Hons) Graphic Design at AUB in 2017. She is a designer, turned strategist, turned creative hybrid of sorts. Getting under the skin of how things work and how they can work differently has shaped her career so far, currently leading her to work with some of the world's biggest technology brands and their teams.

'Change is needed. Diverse design teams can have more creativity, fresher ideas and a bigger impact.

If you are kicking off a career in the creative industry, know that you have a voice and can lead wherever you find yourself.'

Discover your passion

Be user-led

Find a mentor

Empower others

Rosie Isbell, Design Director

Tammy Johal graduated from BA (Hons) Graphic Design at AUB in 2016. Tammy is an award-winning conceptual designer who enjoys everything from creating brand identities to crafting campaigns and art directing photoshoots. A driving factor in her work has been encouraging positive social change and challenging stereotypes and perceptions through design. She has been working in London for the past three and a half years. As part of her creative journey, she has worked at BBH, Sunshine, Havas London, MultiAdaptor, Breakthrough and now works fulltime at Philosophy. She has had the chance to work on many exciting projects for clients, notably The Department of Education and United Nations Women.

Izzi Hayes

Tammy Johal

DIVERSE TEAMS = DIVERSE WORK = DIVERSE AUDIENCES

Equal doesn't mean we're all the same. It means we're all **equally respected** for being different. Which means those of us that are helping to create the visual world need to be creating work that can speak to, represent, and empower everyone's differences

Izzi Hays
Creative strategist
MultiAdaptor

'As a female British Indian designer, the overwhelming lack of diversity in the creative industries has actually pushed me to speak up, know my worth and realise that I can be that person who represents the next generation of talent.'

T Levels Branding & Campaign

Tammy Johal
Mid-weight Designer
Philosophy

I have attended every single one of
the events organised by AUB Human
this year and they all helped me to see
the world from a new perspective,
to be more empathetic and aware
of things happening around me.
**The event that had the biggest impact
on me was to celebrate 'International
Women's Day' with alumni from
the Graphic Design course.**
The personal stories the alumni shared
regarding possible career barriers as
well as recommendations of how to
overcome them, really affected me.
I am looking forward to all the
AUB Human events next year!

Simona Dimitrova
Student

SEVRA DAVIS

Since the beginning, AUB Human has asked
challenging questions about how design and
creativity can most effectively bring about
positive change to the most pressing social,
environmental and economic issues we face
today. By not only highlighting important issues
but also demonstrating positive change 'in
action' through the work of designers and
creatives from a range of industries, the AUB
Human initiative has helped to stimulate debate
and inspire a generation.

I have dedicated my career to the positive
potential of what design can do and the role
of education in shifting this; the inception
and realisation of AUB Human has been an
inspiring companion in my own journey, long
may it continue.

Sevra Davis is Director of Architecture Design and
Fashion at the British Council, responsible for creating
new opportunities for the UK design sector around the
world through collaboration and exchange.

POLLUTION PODS

Installation
October 2019

'Pollution Pods was commissioned by NTNU as part of Climart, a four-year research project that examines the underlying psychological mechanisms involved in both the production and reception of visual art, using these findings in an attempt to unite the natural sciences to the visual arts.

Five interconnected geodesic domes contain carefully mixed recipes emulating the relative presence of ozone, particulate matter, nitrogen dioxide, sulphur dioxide and carbon monoxide which pollute London, New Delhi, San Paolo and Beijing. Starting from a coastal location in Norway, the visitor passes through increasingly polluted cells, from dry and cold locations to hot and humid.' (Pinsky, 2020)

Photo: Pollution Pods on Brownsea Island [Michael Pinsky]

MICHAEL PINSKY'S POLLUTION PODS

AUB Human was delighted to play a part in enabling Michael Pinsky's ground-breaking installation, Pollution Pods, to be sited on Brownsea Island, Dorset.

The Pollutions Pods are a series of interlinked geodesic domes, that give visitors an opportunity to walk through the atmosphere in each separate pod which recreates the air quality, smell and temperature of five major cities – Tautra, London, Beijing, São Paulo and New Delhi.

Creator Michael Pinsky said: 'In the Pollution Pods, I have tried to distil the whole bodily sense of being in each place. For instance, being in São Paulo seems like a sanctuary compared to New Delhi, until your eyes start to water from the sensation of ethanol, whilst Tautra is unlike any air you'll have ever breathed before, it is so pure.'

Alice Stevens, AUB Human founder, who suggested the National Trust Brownsea Island site for the Pollution Pods, was instrumental in AUB's part in the collaboration between Activate, producers of Inside Out Dorset, the county's biennial outdoor arts festival, and Cape Farewell, the artist-led organisation that uses culture to change how people think about climate change. The presentation of Pollution Pods on Brownsea Island in October has been part-funded by AUB, Dorset Council and Arts Council England, supported by the Cultural Hub, and hosted by National Trust.

Students from six undergraduate programmes at AUB visited the installation to undertake a number of projects inspired by the Pollution Pods, including a graphic design project based on environmental data, as well as field work in areas of creative writing, design, costume and architecture.

Photo: Entering London [Michael Pinsky]

This art installation raises very important and pertinent questions about our climate

Kate Wood
Activate

Professor Mary Oliver, AUB's Dean of Media and Performance, said: 'AUB is proud to be partners in bringing this significant artwork to Brownsea Island in order to draw attention to the issue of global pollution.'

Kate Wood, Executive & Artistic Director of Activate, added: 'This art installation raises very important and pertinent questions about our climate and to be able to present it in such an iconic natural location as Brownsea Island offers a place where we can think about our impact locally and globally'

Olivia Gruitt, Visitor Experience and Volunteering Manager at National Trust, Brownsea Island, said: 'We've done a lot of engagement around the impact of climate change on Brownsea Island, especially around sea levels rising, and we're pleased now to be shining a light on air quality. The National Trust is taking significant measures to reduce its carbon footprint but everyone has a role to play in this and we hope that this thought-provoking project will help people understand that the air we breathe needs protecting from excess pollutants.'

Nearly 3,000 people experienced the Pollution Pods on Brownsea Island over the four days at the end of October and it received considerable media attention on BBC Radio Solent and BBC TV live, as well as in print.

Prior to arriving in Dorset, the Pollution Pods, which have been at the centre of continued calls for action over climate change, were sited in New York at the UN Climate Action Summit in September 2019. Whilst in New York, the domes were visited by climate activist Greta Thunberg, who heard first-hand from Michael Pinsky how the atmosphere in each pod recreates the air quality, smell and temperature of the five cities.

Nearly 3,000 people experienced the Pollution Pods on Brownsea Island.

BUILDING THE POLLUTION PODS

Natalie Carr, AUB Human Intern and BA (Hons) Graphic Design graduate, talks through her experience building Michael Pinsky's Pollution Pods on Brownsea Island.

It was a cold October morning when I made my way to the Sandbanks ferry terminal to get a boat to Brownsea Island. The volunteer build team (as we became known), were greeted by Dom Kippin from Activate, the co-presenters of the Pollution Pods on Brownsea Island. After a short trip across Poole Harbour on the National Trust boat, we arrived on the island feeling excited and a little anxious, not knowing quite what was in store for us. For me, it was also my first time on Brownsea. Others were well accustomed to its fairy-tale-esque feel, with peacocks, deer, chickens and red squirrels greeting us inquisitively in search of food.

We met the team from Cape Farewell; Ant, Cleo, Dan and Berry, who had travelled across the world with the Pollution Pods, building them from Melbourne to New York with professionals and volunteers alike. We were given tasks and worked in teams following the carefully planned out

We were cold, wet, blistered and bruised... but we did it!

instructions for each stage of the pods build, and it soon became a competition for who could get their pod constructed the quickest! I teamed up with Clare, an AUB alumni from MA Fine Art, and we worked rhythmically around our first pod and quickly moved onto a second. The sun began to warm and the dew on the field disappeared. Ed Ward, AUB Interior Architecture lecturer; Omar, BA Architecture student and Chris, AUB alumni and Inside Out Dorset volunteer, began to fill giant black pipes with gravel. This was a laborious and dirty job but it left Clare and I to assemble the final pods.

The second day was colder and darker than the first. Cloud cover blocked the sun, making the island feel gloomy. Our challenge was to build connecting tunnels between the five pods. We worked our way through another set of sticks and another set of instructions. Progress felt slow and our hands were chapped, but the linings of the pods were going in; huge tent-like plastics fastened to ring nuts with a combination of bungees, balls and cable ties. It was a painstaking process and the plastics wreaked of the 'pollution' that was soon to fill the pods. After what felt like a very long day, we left the island, leaving the Cape Farewell team to another half-hour of work before darkness set in

The final build day. Wiring snaked between the pods and simulated pollution generating machines went into each pod, each specific to the cities' pollution, temperature and humidity. Time was slipping away and the rain soon descended. The tables to hold the screens displaying pollution information in each of the five locations was being assembled in the downpour whilst the rest of the teams' jobs enjoyed the protection of the pods. The Cape Farewell team still had work to do but for us, our final day was over. We legged it to the ferry once more and expelled tired sighs of relief that the work was done. It had been hard, we were cold, wet, blistered and bruised. But we did it.

Arriving on the island once more, this time with the Pollution Pods fully functional and open to the public, each pod emitted an undeniable odour with the temperature, visibility and humidity being distinct, London reminding me of London, New Delhi reminding me of New Delhi.

Michael Pinsky's Pollution Pods certainly are an impressive immersive installation that really make you reflect on the world's air quality. I feel very proud to have had the opportunity to assist in building and experiencing the installation.

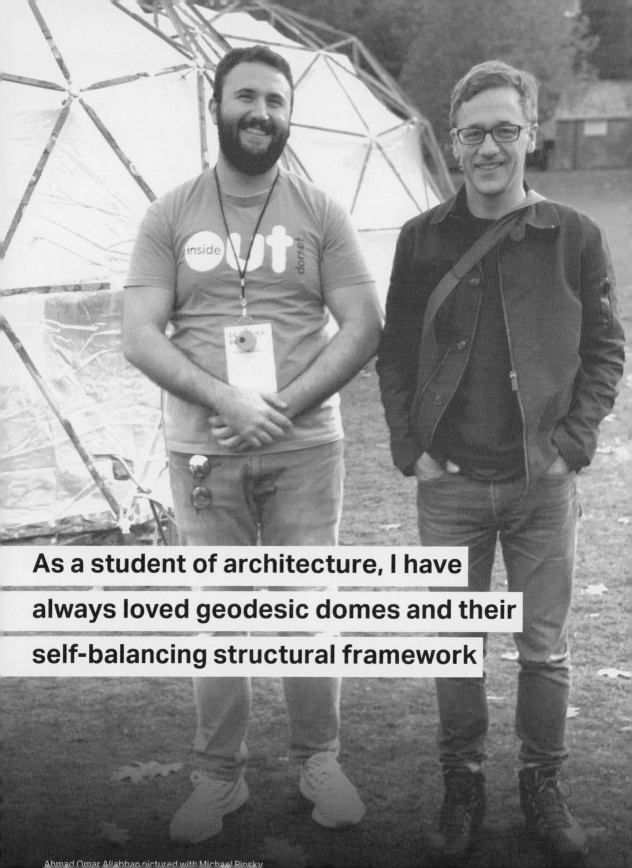

As a student of architecture, I have always loved geodesic domes and their self-balancing structural framework

SIMPLE QUICK CONSTRUCTION

Ahmad Omar Aljabban, BA (Hons) Architecture

When the opportunity to get involved with constructing this globally important installation by the artist Michael Pinsky, it was too good to miss.

Volunteering in the construction of the Pollution Pods and the responsibility of guiding visitors around once constructed, provided me with the experience of interacting directly with the audience. I was able to discover the immediate sensory responses and reactions to the physical conditions represented in each dome. This offered me further insights relating to my own research into sensory architecture and material making.

Practically, the technical ability to chemically reproduce the smell and varying air densities was fascinating to learn. The process involved a bespoke machine to generate the environmental conditions from dome to dome. This links directly to my research in how to invoke a place through olfactory experience.

Over the three days of volunteering, the practical experience of construction in collaboration with others from multidisciplinary backgrounds in the arts was really enjoyable. Everyone brought their own method and imagination to the facilitation of the whole process. The whole experience has been positive, learning more about simple quick and effective construction techniques which can be applied to self-assembly. Also, in a more personal way, observing how the experience of being in a simulated polluting city was more meaningful to the participants as it was a direct sensation, the outcome being that people might take more responsibility for climate change because the reality was very immediate.

+

CLIMATE IN CRISIS

To align with Michael Pinsky's installation on Brownsea Island, Activate Performing Arts, producers of Inside Out Dorset, invited the public to join a panel discussion: Climate in Crisis—Can Art Inspire Action?

The event, chaired by Alice Stevens, AUB Human Founder, included the artist, Michael Pinsky, Molly Scott Cato, Green Party MEP and Ruth Andrade, Responsible for Regenerative Impact & Charitable Giving at Lush.

The discussion was in response to the Pollution Pods around climate change, pollution and air quality but the debate was broad, ranging from the effectiveness of XR's Creative Rebellion interventions, to the effects that BREXIT could have on the environment and the importance of art as protest in making a difference,

encouraging receptiveness of ideas and spurring engagement and action. Alice Stevens said: 'I was excited to be chairing an event that enabled us to debate how creativity, such as the Pollution Pods, can facilitate audience engagement with complex environmental issues and play a pivotal role in driving forward action over climate change.'

Over seventy people, including members of the public, BCP council, local artists, and AUB students and staff, attended the free panel discussion event at the Lighthouse, Poole's Centre for the Arts.

Can Art Inspire Action?

As artists and designers, our graduates will play a significant role in both shaping the debates around climate change and designing solutions to abate its harmful effects

Prof. Mary Oliver
Dean of the Faculty: Media and Performance

CHRISTIAN MCLENING

While design may at first appear to us as the artefact, design as tangible product, the real power of design is the impact it can have on us as humans, on our society. This human aspect of design is the great strength of design creativity to make change for good.

AUB Human embraces the ethos that creativity has the capacity to make real change to people's lives through design, indeed it recognises the profound responsibility and honour it is to design for our fellow humans. The AUB Human initiative is at the very heart of the AUB community. AUB Human is grown from a desire to explore the potential we all have as creatives and also to share with others beyond our campus the passion and joy that creativity can bring to the world.

Think AUB Human, think transformative change.

Dr. Christian McLening
Dean of School: Art, Design and Architecture

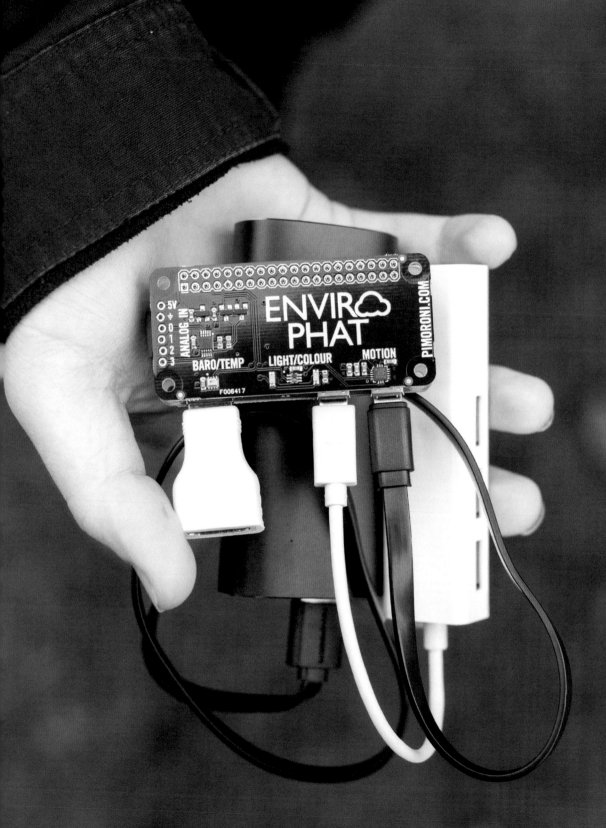

BROWNSEA ISLAND DATA COLLECTION

Taking inspiration from the Pollution Pods, second year BA (Hons) Graphic Design students were challenged with communicating an environmental point of view based on the problems they identified through the collection of data.

Using various methods of data collection, from Raspberry Pis to sound recordings, students gathered data from a range of sources such as noise pollution, water samples, commuting patterns to documenting bio-indicators such as lichen. Subsequently, students were asked if they could mitigate the problem they identified through innovative design thinking. Solutions varied from giant interactive water purifying sculptures to store labels that had clearer information about a garment's ethical and carbon footprint.

The short, eight-day project culminated in a pop-up studio exhibition and was attended by industry professionals including Producer Dom Kippin from arts organisation, Inside Out Dorset.

Students sampled environmental data, using creative coding to explore novel forms of data visualisation

Mark Osborne
Senior Lecturer

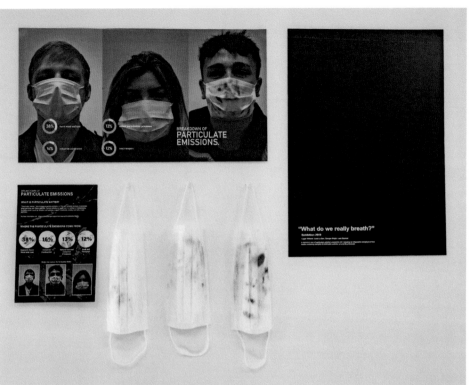

Our original model was a take on a kitchen
Rainwater would pass through the large-scale
being filtered as it did so. It would then fall into
container below where it would be processed in
order to make it safe to consume.

STUDENT WORK RECOGNISED IN CREATIVE CONSCIENCE AWARDS 2020

AUB Human was delighted to attend the virtual Creative Conscience Awards celebration on 28th September 2020 which saw presentations from Sir Jonathon Porritt and Chrissy Levett. Students from BA (Hons) Architecture, Graphic Design, Illustration, Fashion and Visual Communication were thrilled to have their work recognised in these prestigious international awards.

Alice Stevens, AUB Human founder, said: 'The philosophy of Creative Conscience is similar to that of our own, so we feel very proud that students from courses across the AUB campus have achieved so highly in these awards that aim to benefit the environment and communities in which we live and work'.

Marion Morrison, Course Leader for BA (Hons) Graphic Design said: 'The Creative Conscience award winners showcased in this publication allow us to demonstrate how our AUB Graphic Design students, have mastered a set of design skills that can be applied to leverage innovative creative thinking, as a means to tackle a wider range of challenging problems, and to create positive change.

We cultivate the talents of our designers, encouraging them to define appropriate research methods for understanding and exploring new user needs and preferences. We do this by using teaching practices involving iterative steps, open discussion, research, prototyping and experiments. In this process we gain insight into unfamiliar contexts and explore opportunities to turn user needs into human centred solutions'.

A few of the Creative Conscience Award winners are featured on the following pages, but please look at the website to see all the AUB award winners from 2020: aub.ac.uk/aub-human/aub-human-awards

PURIFY

Olivia Simpson, Katie Bridge, Sophie Corbin & Holly Gray
BA (Hons) Graphic Design

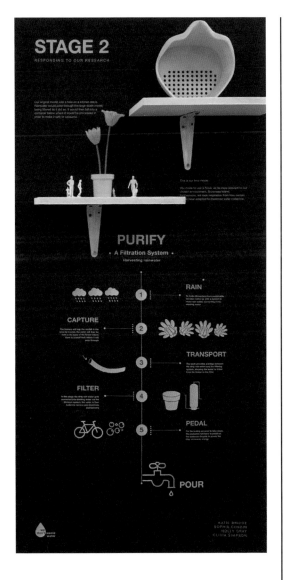

Inspired by a visit to Michael Pinsky's installation, Pollution Pods on Brownsea Island, Olivia, Katie, Sophie and Holly have designed a unique rainwater harvesting and filtration system to reduce water wastage on the island.

Olivia, a second year student, tells us: 'Taking the idea from nature, we designed a giant flower that collected the rainwater. The flower would not only look beautiful, but be functional, making people want to drink from this natural filtration system'.

Katie adds: 'Our project was focused on creating a positive environmental impact and having others recognise this is very motivating and inspiring for us.'

Purify received the Bronze Award in the Graphic Design category.

SNEAKARMA

Tom Cornwell
BA (Hons) Graphic Design

Sneakarma is a sustainable shoe leasing service that aims to change the current model of fashion from a linear approach to circular.

Shoes are an increasingly major contributor to the current environmental crisis, with 24.2 billion pairs of footwear made in 2018 alone (World footwear, 2019).

Tom says: 'The fashion industry has a huge role to play in the world becoming more sustainable and I believe the first step to achieving this is to challenge the norms of ownership'.

Tom was pleased to receive the Highly Commended award for 'Sneakarma' in the Service Design category.

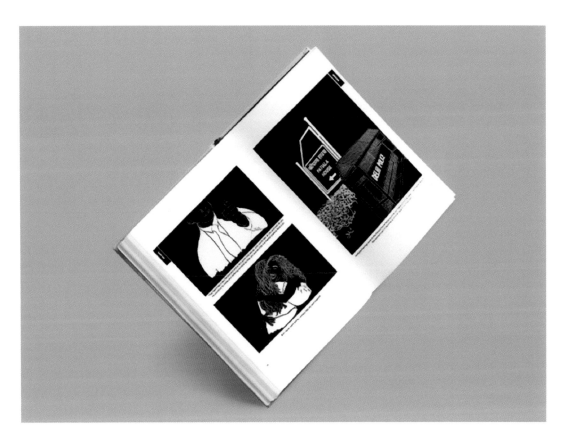

LOG KYA KHENGE?

Namrata Chandra
BA (Hons) Visual Communication

Log Kya Khenge? is Hindi for 'What Will People Say?'. In her graphic novel, Namrata displays the stories of four divorced Indian women and their relationships with society.

Namrata's project received the Bronze Award in the Illustration category.

THE GLASSWORKS

Anna Freiesleben
BA (Hons) Architecture

The Glassworks responds to contemporary narratives on migration. The panes of fused glass form a series of flexible, sliding screens, allowing visitors and artists to literally 'cross boundaries' and exhibit personal narratives from across the world.

Anna won Silver in the Architecture, Engineering & Interior Design category.

LADY GARDEN

Sophie McPherson, Mary Hart, Stella Bonova & Neisha Rendel
BA (Hons) Fashion & Illustration

Lady Garden is an illustrative publication highlighting the importance of female intimate hygiene and self-care.

Sophie from BA (Hons) Fashion, collaborated with students from BA (Hons) Illustration, Mary, Stella and Neisha to create the publication that showcases the 'Lush Me' range. The students were delighted to win the Bronze award in the Illustration category.

NUALA CLARKE

It has been our pleasure to watch AUB Human grow, and with it the placement of sustainability at the forefront of AUB.

AUB Human has engaged our community with environmental and ethical issues through innovative campaigns, exhibitions, and events, encouraging a shift toward more conscious thinking. AUB Students' Union has enjoyed collaborating with AUB Human over the past few years and hope to continue to share ideas and work together to inspire our students to be passionate, aware global citizens.

Nuala Clarke
Activities & Communities Coordinator
AUB Students' Union

TREE PLANTING VOLUNTEER DAY

On Sunday 1st December 2019, with support from the Woodland Trust, AUBSU went to Upton Country Park to plant over 1,000 trees to help support the local green spaces.

SUSTAINABLE FUTURES

Exhibition
February - April 2020

AUB Human was pleased to present Sustainable Futures, an exhibition of student work from across the university campus that seeks to find creative solutions to the global climate crisis we are currently facing, and to address the UN Sustainable Development Goals.

The exhibition showcased a broad range of student work, from those that promote responsible and ethical consumption to ideas that work in harmony with natural ecosystems in addressing the challenges of creating more sustainable cities. The exhibition also included winning work from the 2019 AUB Sustainability Awards as selected by the Environment Committee.

The exhibition was curated by Natalie Carr, AUB Human graduate intern and co-curated by James Jackson, Senior Campus Services Officer and Alice Stevens, AUB Human.

Consumerism is Killing the Earth

Cynthia Porta Fernandez
& Dominikus Kronwitter
BA (Hons) Graphic Design

A short animated sequence based on an article by Andy Coghlan in the New Scientist titled: Consumerism is 'eating the future'.

The sequence also promotes Buy Nothing Day, which is a movement celebrated in over sixty countries that aims to encourage people to shop less.

AUB Human presents

Sustainable Futures

24th February – 1st April 2020
South House Reception

Sustainable Futures is an exhibition of student work from across the university that seeks to find creative solutions to the global climate crisis we are facing, and to address the UN Sustainable Development Goals. The exhibition showcases student projects that work in harmony with natural ecosystems, address the challenges in creating more sustainable cities to promoting responsible and ethical consumption. The exhibition also includes the Environment Committee selections for the 2019 AUB Sustainability Awards.

AUB Human celebrates social, ethical and sustainable creative practice whilst also curating debate and challenging ways of thinking, doing and making in addressing how creativity can make a positive global difference. AUB human brings together designers, architects, artists, filmmakers and other practitioners who share a desire to bring about positive change through creative practice.

Thank you to BA (Hons) Fashion and BA (Hons) Graphic Design for their support.

SUSTAINABLE DEVELOPMENT GOALS

AUB SUSTAINABILITY AWARDS

These awards are in recognition of final year student work that takes a particularly innovative approach to sustainability, as awarded by the Environment Committee.

I was pleased to be featured in the Sustainable Futures exhibition with my project, A Healing School. My ideas continue to be influenced by AUB Human, including talks by Mark Chivers and Ram Shergill as part of the New Narratives symposium. For me, these speakers brought innovative aspects of sustainability to the fore, inspiring me to think from alternative design perspectives in developing my projects and future thinking.

Charley Harvey
BA (Hons) Architecture

Charley Harvey, BA (Hons) Architecture

An elementary school renovation in Seoul, South Korea, that aims to actively heal its inhabitants, reducing mental and physical illness internally, sending ripples of health through the wider community.

The project proposes a precedent of sustainable design, from employing natural ventilation strategies to using a green roof to reduce the urban heat island effect of Seoul, increasing biodiversity in the city setting, and reusing existing structure and materials.

Using natural forms and materials are the underlying elements of the project, following the biophilic design method: designing for human's innate need to be close to nature and the life forms within. By designing with the relationship between the natural world and humans, architecture can be made to benefit both.

A PLATFORM FOR JOY

Natasha Fry, BA (Hons) Interior Architecture

The design proposes to purge the uncommunicative, dissociated environment of station users, and bring back a relationship between this gateway building and the city.

A Platform for Joy proposes a joyful, narrative experience through the train station, which naturally facilitates the forming of relationships and connections between its diverse users.

The design uses symbolism within its architecture to reinforce its core aims of forming relationships: drawing on the overlap of natural and built environments, interior and exterior worlds, the building and its surrounding city, and human tendencies and nature.

Ana Clark Ribeiro, BA (Hons) Textiles

Ana worked with natural fibres, organic processes and reusing second-hand clothing to create a collection that encompasses her story through sustainable processes.

Ana tells us, 'Through drawing, collages and stitch I aim to capture the raw and natural beauty of the world around us. Growing up in Brazil, I had the luxury of being surrounded by nature and therefore, I have constantly found myself returning to such natural environments and being inspired'.

Course Leader Anne Marie Howatt added, 'Ana has been committed to investigating sustainability within textile practice during her 3rd year. She has utilised upcycled fabrics, developed vegetable dying processes and has an awareness of water waste and usage'.

LA, REPRISE

Molly Board, BA (Hons) Fashion

La, Reprise is a sustainable collection for men who have an ethical awareness of the modern world. La, Reprise sees the beauty in the discarded; the resource in what others regard as 'waste'.

Molly worked with the local community, using waste materials and second-hand clothes from local charity shops, in the creation of new garments.

OFF THE GRID

Ella Rose, BA (Hons) Commercial Photography

Off the Grid is an exploration and documentation of different methods and ways to live a sustainable lifestyle. To live off the grid is to reside in a home that is not connected to mains gas, electricity, phone lines, water and sewage.

Ella's project aims to raise awareness of the current environmental issues we face, creating a wider understanding of how important sustainable living is for our generation.

GAIA : TRACK YOUR EMISSIONS

Rania Qaddoura, BA (Hons) Graphic Design

GAIA: Track Your Emissions explores whether as a society we can change our eating behaviours to reduce our impact on climate change.

GAIA is a climate footprint tracker that consumers would use to monitor their carbon emissions, but also acts as an educational and functional tool, providing plant-based recipes to aid the transition to eating less meat.

JAMES JACKSON

AUB Human is not just a highlight of academic excellence but an extremely vital tool in a holistic approach to EcoCampus and Fairtrade as well as a staple of the Environment Committee's progressive and innovative thinking.

In 2020 AUB achieved Fairtrade status and EcoCampus platinum award.

James Jackson
Senior Campus Services Officer

Ethics and Creative Practice

Symposium in support of Global Ethics Day

On 16th October AUB Human was delighted to bring together industry professionals for an afternoon of inspirational talks in support of Global Ethics Day 2019.

The Ethics and Creative Practice symposium explored the role of ethics in an interconnected world and confronted the issues that face creatives both personally and professionally. Here at Arts University Bournemouth, we are committed to the provision of a working and learning environment founded on dignity, respect and equity. AUB is dedicated to the highest standards of research integrity and has confirmed its commitment to comply fully with the Universities UK Concordat to support Research Integrity.

Convenor: Alice Stevens
Co-convenor: Mark Osborne

ETHICS

SPEAKERS

Pali Palavathanan is Co-Founder and Creative Director of TEMPLO, a branding and digital agency based in London, specialising in #CreativityForChange. TEMPLO's work focuses on human rights, education, culture and ethical businesses with a current client list that includes the United Nations, Migrant Help, Amnesty International, Tate Modern and the Design Museum. TEMPLO's work has been featured in Wired Magazine, The Independent, on the Channel 4 News, and in the 'What Design Can Do' book 'Designing for Activism' and was recently exhibited at London's Design Museum as part of the 'Hope to Nope' exhibition about graphic design and politics.

Ted Hunt is an independent speculative/discursive/critical designer living and working in London and currently a resident of Somerset House Studios. Ted's work investigates the intersections between our ancient behavioural-driven selves and modern technologically-driven selves. He continually explores non-linear/alternative paradigms and examines the boundaries between subjective, objective and inter-subjective interpretations and perspectives.

Laura Yarrow is a Senior UX consultant at Experience UX. She has spent the last 13 years in the digital industry, first as a web developer and eventually moving into user experience design, fuelled by a growing curiosity about the people she was creating products and services for. Her passions are ethnographic and field research, soft skills for UX practitioners, behavioural psychology and understanding people.

Paul Wenham-Clarke is an Association of Photographers Gold Award winner and a Professor of Photography at Arts University Bournemouth, where he runs the MA Commercial Photography course. What links his work is a strong desire to communicate with the public on social and environmental issues that he feels passionate about. Whether it is loss of human and animal life on our roads, or, as in the case of his latest book Urban Gypsies, a community fighting to protect its cultural identity. His documentary work often asks us to consider topics that are virtually on our doorstep.

As designers we occupy an incredibly privileged position of influencing and shaping the world around us with the designs and solutions we create. How can we start to adhere to a digital code of ethics to ensure our impact on humanity is a positive one?

Laura Yarrow
Senior UX consultant
Experience UX

How can we start to adhere to a digital code of ethics?

OUR IMPACT AS DESIGNERS

As designers we fail every day to understand the people we are designing for. Digital services and apps that are addictive. Photographs in the media that cut out those from minority backgrounds to frame only those the photographer identifies with. Products that are designed only for those that are able bodied or have a particular colour of skin. The list is endless.

Often, we can forget that as designers we operate in a privileged position of being able to impact the world around us – for better or worse. It might seem like the work you do has a small effect, but it's much more complex than that. Consider the photograph you have taken, the artwork created or piece you have written – who will see that? What emotions will it evoke in them? Can it harm them? Can they use it properly? Does this work seek to exclude or repress anyone?

The ability to critique and ask probing, candid questions of our work is one of the most important skills we can start to hone as the world changes ever more rapidly, becoming more connected, complex and turbulent. And to become great designers that promote positive change, we need to become aware of the interconnectedness of our work to society, and see it located as an intricately linked part within a much larger whole.

I believe that designers have an ethical remit to ensure that the work they create is well considered to 'first do no harm' to the humans that will use or experience our work

Laura Yarrow
Experience UX

USERS ARE.. / PEOPLE ARE..

A seismic social shift has taken place seeing much of humanity evolve from a person to a user. We are all complicit in this shift. We have collectively accepted this new social contract unchallenged. We 'agreed' to it. We perpetuate and propagate it.

We are now the users, the using and the used.

USERS ARE.. / PEOPLE ARE..

USERS ARE..	PEOPLE ARE..
Logical and predictable	Superstitious and romantic
In need of products & services	Seeking opportunity & recognition
Continually generating metadata	Continually creating relationships
Driven by the security of certainty	Habitualised to anxiety and doubt
Content with binary choices	Evolved to adapt to complexity
Motivated by frictionless existence	Existing in the coarse reality of society
in need of 'solutions' to problems	Coping with / living with problems
Stakeholders	Of little investment in systems
Of presupposed capacity	Capable of transcending limits
Products of capitalism	Products of human evolution
Awaiting options	Creating alternatives
Monetizable	Indebted to social exchanges
Quantifiable	Exhibiting highly unpredictable traits
Easily pleased	Complex and troubled

Ted Hunt
Independent Designer

THE IMPORTANCE OF TRUST

Paul Wenham-Clarke
Professor of Photography

Strong documentary photography is often based on access to places and lives that others are denied. These people are often very wary of photographers for good reason.

Historically we have not been the most empathetic of practitioners, objectifying individuals and casting a sensationalist eye over sensitive issues. However, for me it is vital to build trust and maintain relationships with the participants. Together we make images rather than me taking them. Collaborating with those depicted leads to honest images with genuine narratives that empowers those involved.

Collaborating with those depicted leads to honest images with genuine narratives that empower those involved

Photo: The Urban Gypsies of The Westway (Paul Wenham-Clarke)

The uncomfortable line between making money + staying ethical as a creative

Pali Palavathanan

#CreativityForChange

What is the intention of our design —and what happens after use?

SIMON WIDMER

Ellen MacArthur Foundation

Design out waste and pollution
Keep products and materials in use
Regenerate natural systems

Today, most things are designed for a linear take-make-waste model. Most of what we use we lose. From the clothes we wear to the buildings we live in, to the systems that deliver our food, we tolerate that most of what we create ends up in landfills and incinerators.

The circular economy provides us with a different vision — a model that works in the long-run. A model that is regenerative and that builds on three principles:

- Design out waste and pollution
- Keep products and materials in use
- Regenerate natural systems

Transitioning towards a circular economy is one of the biggest creative challenges of our time and it requires new mindsets and design approaches.

The good news is that pioneers all over the world show that it is possible. And we can get started too. We can use new emerging tools and resources. We can connect with others on the journey and learn from each other. We can ask ourselves: What is the intention of our design — and what happens to it after use? How does it fit into the big picture? How can we apply circular economy principles in whatever we create?

Biography:
Simon Widmer is the Design Network and Creative Lead at the Ellen MacArthur Foundation. He believes in the power of design and our ability to creatively shape products, services and systems for a positive future.

AUB Human

Lockdown Takeover

STUDENTS SHOWCASE WORK ON INSTAGRAM

The takeover event culminated on Thursday 14th May 2020 at the height of the Covid-19 pandemic. It gave students from wherever they were in the world an opportunity to come together, network and showcase their recent work on Instagram.

The Graphic Design students had been challenged with a choice of social or environmental projects—to design a packaging system that reduces the emissions, food and material waste footprint of a range of supermarket projects to zero, or to collaborate with BA (Hons) Interior Architecture students to design a wayfinding system for people with dementia living in a care home setting.

Alice Stevens, AUB Human founder, said: 'Although Covid-19 has been a game changer, we have been delighted to see how resourceful the students have been in tackling these complex briefs during lockdown. Although collaborating from their own homes, they have shown resilience, determination and ambition. Students have produced some truly innovative solutions to these global challenges of food packaging and ageing populations, demonstrating how design can make a positive difference to pressing environmental and societal needs.'

Natalie Carr, co-organiser and AUB Human Intern, said: 'It is exciting to be utilising technologies to bring people together from all over the world to celebrate the student work and enable them to network with high profile industry speakers. In the true spirit of AUB Human it is also great to be doing events that have very little environmental impact.'

In addition, the event welcomed nine industry professionals and friends of AUB Human, who shared their experiences of how the Coronavirus Lockdown had affected them both personally and professionally.

INDUSTRY GUESTS

Ruth Andrade, responsible for Regenerative Impact & Charitable Giving at LUSH.

Laura Jordan Bambach, past D&AD President, co-founder of SheSays and Chief Creative Officer at Grey London.

Martin Coyne, founder and Managing Director of Bond + Coyne, an integrated agency that enjoys untangling knotty problems by embracing the unexpected.

Andrea Dell'Anna, senior designer at Human After All, working with industry leaders such as: Uefa, Facebook, The Climate Group, Universal Music and the Italian Ministry of Cultural Heritage.

Umesh Pandya, co-founder of Wayfindr, a multi-award-winning, social tech, not-for-profit that empowers vision impaired people to navigate the world independently. Backed by google.org, Comic Relief and The Big Lottery, Wayfindr became the world's first international standard for audio-based indoor navigation - ITU-T F.921.

Briony Hartley, founder of Goldust Design, a graphic designer, typographer and colour consultant.

Chrissy Levett, Creative Director and TEDx speaker who believes creative thinking is vital for us to solve global challenges. Chrissy is Founder & CEO for Creative Conscience, a global movement set up to inspire, encourage and reward the next generation of creative thinkers to use their talents for social and environmental impact.

Tom Tapper, co-Founder and CEO of Nice and Serious, a B-Corp certified communications agency. Since 2008, Tom has worked with hundreds of international charities and brands to creatively communicate the positive impact they're having on the world.

Paul Willoughby, co-founder and executive creative director at Human After All. An award-winning designer and graphic artist, whose clients include Nike, BAFTA, IBM and Greenpeace. Among other work at Human After All, he handles the creative direction of Weapons of Reason — a project that aims to better articulate and help us understand some of the most complex issues shaping our world.

The world needs creativity now more than ever

Tom Tapper

Nice and Serious

Each of the industry guests awarded a book prize for the project they felt was the most innovative. Umesh Pandya, who has been working in the digital sector for over 18 years, awarded Alexandra Csatari a prize for her project 'Sanum: The Healing Power of Singing'. The project aims to help rehabilitate stroke victims who have Aphasia, which affects the ability to speak and understand what others say. Through the use of technology and gamification, Sanum aims to make repetitive and dull speech therapy exercises more engaging and thus more effective for the users.

Umesh said, 'Alexandra's project has really gone the extra mile to communicate the 'why' and 'how' well, whilst also making the most of the Instagram format to communicate the idea.' Alexandra, who joined the lockdown event from her home in Hungary, told us: 'I have really enjoyed the event, it was so nice to hear all the great feedback and see everyone's work. It has definitely given me more confidence for the future.'

A few of the projects are featured on Instagram.com/aubhuman and the following pages.

It is exciting to be utilising technologies to bring together people from across the world, celebrate the student work and enable them to network with high profile industry speakers

Natalie Carr
AUB Human Intern

HEX YEAH!

Racheal Conceicao, Simona Dimitrova and Cynthia Porta Fernandez

Hex Yeah! Is a new concept in enabling super-markets to become zero waste. The new Hex aisle will be introduced to supermarkets and will enable customers to help the environment whilst also saving money. The system is designed to be as simple as possible.

The concept relies on the containers eventually being composted and returned back to fields to produce more material. The materials we are using in the Hex system are PLA (made from corns) and BeetaPac (sugar beet).

The app will enable customers to scan products' barcodes and see nutritional information, recipes and information about how the product was produced, keep track of the discounts they currently have, and find stores nearby where they can return empty containers or arrange collection.

2nd year student, Cynthia Porta Fernandez said: 'The AUB Human talk by Ruth Andrade from Lush really helped me to look beyond sustainability, into restorative and regenerative design principles. This really inspired me to work harder and find new sustainable solutions to this Future of Packaging project'.

Italian Pasta Salad

👍 91% would make this again

Ingredients

- 1 pound uncooked pasta – I like rotini!
- 3 cups cherry tomatoes, cut in half
- 8 ounces fresh mozzarella cheese balls, cut in half
- 1 lb. salami or summer sausage cut into cubes
- 3/4 cup kalamata olives, sliced
- 3/4 cup pepperoncini (optional, but do it)
- 1/2 cup sliced red onion
- 1/2 cup fresh parsley, chopped

Dressing

COMING
SOON
in stores near you

A Brand new sustainable range, encouraging you to live a reduced-waste lifestyle

HEX FOR LESS, IN JUST THREE STEPS : BUY, USE , RETURN

In just three steps: buy, use, return.

HEX FOR LESS: LESS MONEY, LESS WASTE.

We take care of the rest!

4 FUTURE

Andy Burrow, Amelia Jackson, and Luke Wadwell

4 future is a new eco-friendly brand helping to reduce plastics and packaging. The easily accessible app brings together in-store product information and home eco deliveries whilst gamifying the rewards scheme for customers.

Andy Burrow, 2nd year graphic design student, said: 'During lockdown I began structuring my days around work and found that I became more focussed and productive. The online sessions and tutorials have been easy to access and really helpful, so actually there have been some benefits to lockdown!'

We need radical change in how we buy groceries, we should use Covid-19 as an opportunity to make that change

Luke Wadwell
Student

REFILL

Josh Papps, Dan Trend, Ben Gauge, and Michael Rozen

The UK alone produces more than 170 million tonnes of waste every year, much of it food packaging. Refill aims to solve this by adapting community driven zero-waste systems for use in busy supermarkets. Refill will save both material waste by reusing packaging and food waste, as users will only buy what they need.

By utilising existing food-safe glass jars and integrating them with a new system of lids, Refill allows users to reuse containers they already own, whilst expanding their functionality. An example of which could be adding a spout to a regular glass jar, enabling it to pour liquids.

Subsequently, the 2nd year graphic design students, were pleased to hear that they were winners in the Creative Conscience awards, having been selected from hundreds of entries. Michael Rozen said:

'We are delighted to have won a Creative Conscience award and have our work recognised in this international competition. We hope that we can develop the concept into a reality, helping to save millions of tonnes of waste'.

We are delighted to have won a Creative Conscience award and have our work recognised in this international competition

Michael Rozen
Student

CHRISSY LEVETT

Founder of Creative Conscience

The world will not be destroyed by those who do evil, but by those who watch them without doing anything

—Albert Einstein

Having been inspired by this quote, Chrissy founded Creative Conscience in 2012. She tells us, 'As creatives we have the power to communicate, tell stories, change systems, innovate, to educate society on what we can positively do. We can inspire behavioural change and shift the direction we are currently going'.

'We all have a choice—every action we take makes a difference no matter how small. So let's choose a better way, take ACTion, make every decision count. We can all change the World, one step, one choice at a time'.

AUB HUMAN GAVE ME THE CONFIDENCE TO 'FAIL FAST'

AUB Human has continuously challenged me to think about design in a more critical and innovative way; through participating in workshops, networking and attending talks by industry experts.

This year's 'New Narratives' symposium was particularly formative for my degree final major project. The talk from Rebecca Ford, Head of Design and Innovation at the RSA, was particularly inspiring in pushing my understanding of systems thinking to tackle complex problems and authentically meet user needs. Julian Thompson's (Lead Service Designer at Citizens Advice) talk questioned what is beyond inclusive design, and became even more important to consider with the COVID-19 outbreak, that exposed many issues that designers should be a part of tackling.

The AUB Human speaker events have inspired me and my peers, whilst the workshops follow up this inspiration by enabling students to develop skills and utilise the insights from the talks. An 'Iconothon' workshop, run by Human After All, pushed my skills in communicating complex ideas whilst a workshop with Creative Conscience's Founder, Chrissy Levett, made me excited about further exploring projects that make a difference and progress the debate. AUB Human's network enables students to extend their learning opportunities and build industry contacts. For example, whilst working on BA (Hons) Graphic Design's 2020 virtual graduate showcase, I was able to record a motivating discussion with Chrissy about a designer's role in social change, aiming to inspire others in utilising their skills to make impact.

The range of speakers and workshops have developed my critical thinking skills and provided insights that aided my thesis: which aimed to question if graphic design and visual representations of cultures can ever be non-political.

Motivation from AUB Human events to use my design thinking skills to serve individuals and communities beyond my own, fed into my role leading a local youth group alongside university – opportunities offered through AUB Human gave me the confidence to 'fail fast', especially during lockdown when I had to adapt key services for the youth into virtual formats. Experiences from this time, including the challenge of reaching those without computer access, inspired me to further explore digital literacy and accessibility as a key factor in improving social mobility, especially in a post-COVID society.

I have recently started as a Junior Designer at Battenhall in London – unfortunately this means I have had to step down from my youth leadership position in Bournemouth, but an exciting aspect of this new role is the opportunity to use some of my time for charity work and self-motivated projects.

Isobel Fiske
BA (Hons) Graphic Design

I am delighted to have been accepted onto Creative Conscience's Summer School, which will take the skills and excitement to design for change, ignited in the AUB Human events, even further

VÄLJA

Isobel Fiske
BA (Hons) Graphic Design

**Creating a platform and moment
for difficult conversations.**
A campaign utilising the IKEA brand
and experience to provoke discussion
and thought around organ donation.

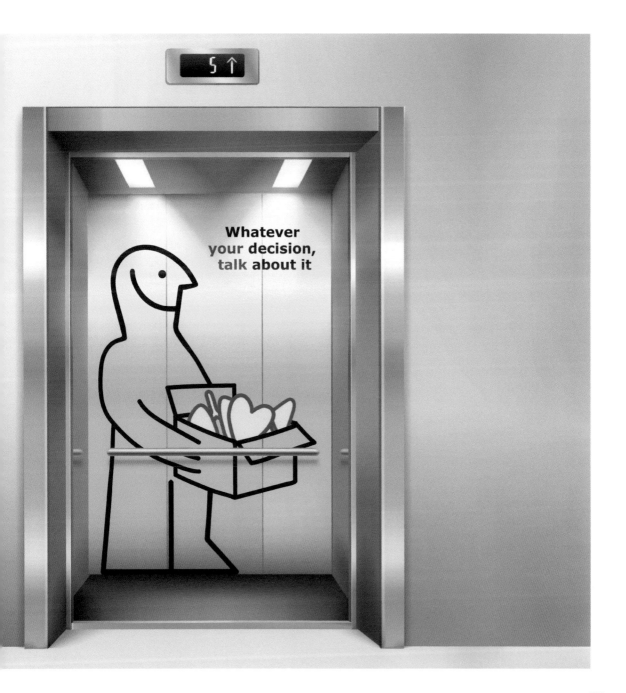

JORDAN BREW

Student, BA (Hons) Graphic Design

AUB Human has helped me to consider how I can change human behaviour to enable a more healthy lifestyle through design thinking. This shift in perspective, (learnt through a great range of lectures), has helped me to think differently and move to an upstream method of thinking, creating subliminal change to a user's mindset to reduce the impact of real-world issues.

I always search for the challenge in my projects looking for an existing issue and identifying a simple alteration to behaviour that with the aid of a successful campaign can create change. The biggest motivation behind taking any projects is environmental observation and discovering more about the given topic, for example with Tandem I noticed the lack of child based rentable bikes within many towns and cities which created a barrier to the accessibility of cycling.

To be rewarded in any category of design is always a great accomplishment, but to be rewarded for projects in a design for good space adds an additional accolade as it creates a bigger communal and environmental impact than just a well-designed piece. If a project can create change or start a discussion, you have achieved so much more.

If a project can create change or start a discussion, you have achieved so much more

Lunch Walks

D&AD New Blood, Pencil
An app redesign with the aim to encourage office workers to get away from their desks at lunch for at least 30 minutes a day.

Tandem Bikes

Nigel Beale prize
The concept of Tandem is to create a platform which allows children to enjoy the same spontaneity and convenience of bike hire.

SUSTAINABILITY AWARDS

The AUB Sustainability Awards are in recognition of final year undergraduate student work that takes a particularly interesting or innovative approach to sustainability. In 2020 the issues and approaches our students took were varied and unique, from creating sustainable events and campaigns to encouraging us to consume less meat, to new shared living models of social sustainability and even a 'veggie' rap musical.

The Environment Committee are responsible for judging the work and panel members are: Jon Reynard, Chair of Environment Committee and University Secretary, James Jackson, Senior Campus Services Officer, Phil Beards, Course leader, Creative Events Management and Alice Stevens, AUB Human Founder.

WINNER

Charley Harvey
BA (Hons) Architecture

Leon Newman & Brianna Barwell
BA (Hons) Acting

HIGHLY COMMENDED

Amelia Best
BA (Hons) Illustration

Tom Cornwell
BA (Hons) Graphic Design

Project team: Earthbourne
BA (Hons) Creative
Events Management

COMMENDED

Ffion McCormack
BA (Hons) Fashion

Emily Duncan
BA (Hons) Fashion Branding
and Communication

Katherine Welch
BA (Hons) Fine Art

Emma Rodak
BA (Hons) Textiles

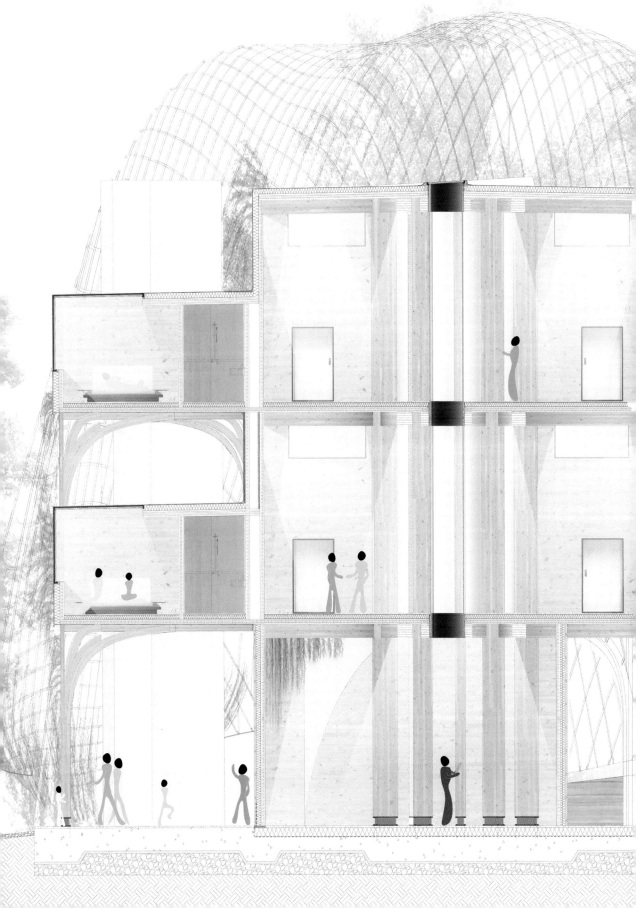

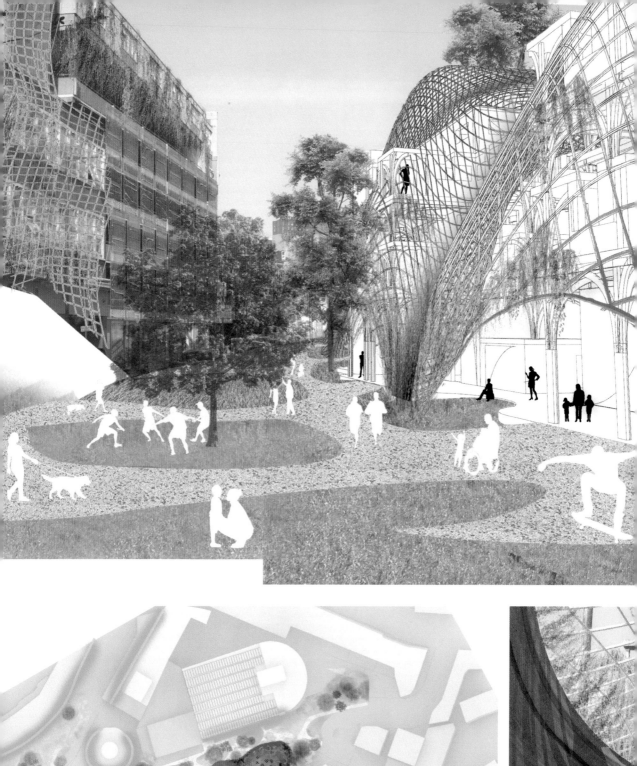

Charley Harvey
BA (Hons) Architecture

Charley's project 'The Urban Chine', proposed a shared living model for Bournemouth town centre, taking its inspiration from the chines landscape and knitting together the living green spaces of the town. The project applies sustainability principles through materiality and technology, as well as aspiring to a new model of social sustainability, merging the natural and built environment.

We asked Charley what winning the award meant to her: 'Sustainability has been at the heart of my projects throughout university and it is a long-held belief that it should be at the heart of all design, as climate change becomes an increasingly prominent issue across the world, having detrimental impacts on society. Being recognised in these awards means the world as it shows AUB is at the forefront of promoting the importance of sustainable design and encourages creative approaches to combatting the climate crisis.'

Charley has since won the Silver Award at the 2020 Creative Conscience Awards for this project in the Architecture, Engineering & Interior Design category.

VEGGIE WRAP

The following is a short extract from Veggie Wrap script written by BA (Hons) Acting student Leon Newman and performed with Brianna Barwell.

Brianna: What if I only buy organic, surely that would be okay?

Leon: Organic farming regulations are designed to grant animals minimal comfort. Organic hens can share one square meter of space with five others. Organic also needs more resources than conventional meat production.

B: More resources? What is more important? Looking after the animals or saving resources?! What if none of this really matters. What if it's true that animals don't have souls and humans do. What if you're completely wrong and animals were put here so that we can eat them. What if that is what I choose to believe. What if I don't care about the animals and only cared about mankind.

L: Beat drops on (man)kind. In 12 years, if mankind doesn't solve the very real issue of climate change, it's effects will be irreversible. Most likely resulting in the extinction of the human race, and many other species. Climate change is also making available water much more erratic. At the core of all of this it is animal agriculture making things problematic. There are 23 billion chickens, 1.5 billion cows, 1 billion pigs and sheep, all on earth right now. 83% of farmland is used for livestock. For example, pasture and farm fodder crops, like corn and soy, together taking up 26% of earth's total land area. The water for the plants grown for meat and dairy production accounts for 27% of global fresh water consumption.

We can't sit and make the assumption that earth can still function. Alfalfa is a common ingredient in cattle feed and just to grow 1kg it takes 510 litres of water, yet the average cow consumes 12kg of feed per day. Divide it all up...

B: Am I about to be surprised by what you're gonna say?

B: Am I about to be surprised by what you're gonna say?

L: One quarter pound hamburger takes around 1650 litres of water. Only a fraction of the nutrients from the fodder crops end up in the meat we buy. See, only 4% of protein, 3% of calories are converted into beef. That is more than 97% of the calories lost to us. Only 18% of the calories humans eat are made up by dairy and meat. We could nourish an additional 3.5 billion humans if we just ate the food we feed to the animals.

B: That is understandable. Wow I can tell you're really on a mission

L: To cut down 15% of greenhouse gas emissions

B: What about the ships, and planes, and trucks, and cars

L: You'll find it's as much as all of those combined.

B: Woah okay that's actually mad, I mean I won't and people won't stop driving or travelling abroad.

L: Of course not, but we all can simply just switch to plant-based meat alternatives, quite a lot of them are scarily meaty, Ha-ha, sorry I got a bit too into that topic, do you want another drink?

One quarter pound hamburger takes around 1650 litres of water. Only a fraction of the nutrients from the fodder crops end up in the meat we buy see. Only 4% of protein, 3% of calories are converted into beef...

We could nourish an additional 3.5 billion humans if we just ate the food we feed to the animals

SAVESOME

Tom Cornwell
BA (Hons) Graphic Design

Tom's project 'Savesome' is a reward scheme for supermarket shoppers aiming to help them reduce their consumption of meat products. The reward scheme encourages users to aim for a healthier meat reduced lifestyle for themselves and for a positive impact on the world around them.

We caught up with Tom to ask how he felt about winning the award. Tom said: 'I just wanted to say thank you for this award, I feel very privileged to be part of this group of students who are all doing amazing things. I have always believed in living life with the aim of leaving the world in a better place than how I found it. The AUB Human Talks inspired me to take action in my work and the insightful projects became the catalyst for my own ideas. With the ecological crisis we are now facing, innovative design is needed to create a sustainable future for our planet and the life it supports.'

Tom has since been asked to speak about his work at the Service Design Fridge Festival in London, September 2020.

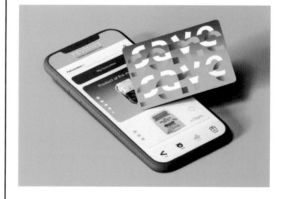

savesome

Savesome is a reward scheme for supermarket shoppers aiming to reduce their consumption of meat products.

Less meat

more rewards

Scan to start saving

EARTH-BOURNE

BA (Hons) Creative Events Management

EarthBourne was formed by a group of Creative Events Management students with the aim of educating children and promoting the impact of climate change in a peaceful and positive way.

EarthBourne at Home, released after Earth Hour on the 21st April 2020, was designed as a website packed full of free activities and ideas to help families celebrate our incredible Earth. Crafts from recycled items, gardening without a garden, nature-themed yoga and exciting edible goodies made from basic ingredients are just a few of the things that were featured on the website.

EarthBourne Student Team: Georgina Mason, Catherine Mackenzie, Isabel Garcia-Godoy, Luc Perez, Nicola Sadler and Charlie Wright.

THE AIR WE BREATHE

Amelia Best
BA (Hons) Illustration

Amelia's project is a beautifully illustrated fictional children's picture book. The book, titled 'The Air we Breathe', is based on air pollution and how we can help our planet to overcome it.

LIFE AFTER LAKE

Ffion McCormack
BA (Hons) Fashion

Ffion's accessories collection, 'Life After Lake', takes inspiration from her family's impassioned admiration of water skiing. When we asked Ffion if she could explain further, she told us: 'My parents' cringe-worthy wedding was the spark of this idea; as they left the alter under an archway of water skis to then be towed away on the back of a speed boat, I felt this wedding was iconic and had to be shared!'

Pioneering the reworking of vibrant, surplus fabric is a conscious work ethic behind the collection ensuring there is a life after the lake.

Ffion continues: 'Reusing existing materials is extremely beneficial and important to not only me as a designer but also the environment. Each accessory in this collection was created from reusing and reclaiming vintage wetsuits; life jackets, water shoes, knee board straps and more all from the late 1980's to the early 2000's, donated by close family and friends. I wanted to keep the originality and character of each wetsuit or life jacket alive within every design.'

WEEKEND BAG

SOLACE IN NATURE

Emma Rodak
BA (Hons) Textiles

Through an exploration of the relationship between nature in design, this ecologically conscious collection is aimed for the couture market. The concept of Biophilia suggests that because we evolved in nature, we have a biological need to connect with it. As we are in a new era of combating mass species extinction and climate change, seeking solace in nature has never been so important. Inspiration is captured from the Japanese tradition Shinrin Yoku, a form of eco-therapy that reconnects humans to nature through the act of forest bathing.

The visual imagery is collected from my favourite childhood place, Swithland Wood where the high-end, plant-based fibres used within the collection are reflective of the organic imagery of the woods. A combination of valued hand techniques that contrast against contemporary digital techniques are varied throughout the collection. With a focus on delicate embellishment and tactile surface textures, this will, I hope, create a natural sense of touch and bring joy to the consumer with an intention to re-connect them with nature through the plant-based, sustainable fibres used for the high-end market.

JAMES 2:5

Katherine Weltch
BA (Hons) Fine Art

Katherine works with materials that she found in specific locations, recycling them and using their inherent meaning to transmit her ideas.

Two works were created to put across the idea of how sociopolitical and socioeconomical factors affect the people and cultural norms of the Dominican Republic. The country is often viewed solely as a tourist destination, which overlooks the fact that there is an insurmountable amount of petty crime, violence, unstable homes and alcohol addiction.

James 2:5

Dimensions Variable – Installation (May 2020): Palm tree fronds, five plantains, two coconuts, two machetes, three beer bottles, Brugal rum, pestle and mortar, Spanish bible open to James 2:5, painted breezeblocks, and a dried calabash.

WHY AUB HUMAN?

Simon Beeson
Course Leader, BA (Hons)
Architecture (ARB/RIBA Part 1)

Why AUB Human? At a time when all aspects of our lives are commodified and where graduates are mere economic units, our learning community asks the simple question: there has to be more to life than this? And at least part of the answer at AUB is AUB Human. Under this umbrella we can explore the wider consequences of our education, creative practice and our lives. Connecting our actions to the consequences of our actions needs to be fundamental to critical thinking and critical making. In BA Architecture, we began the year by watching Greta Thunberg's speech to the 2019 UN Climate Action Summit in New York. She asks: 'We are at the beginning of a mass extinction and all you can talk about is money and fairy tales of eternal economic growth – how dare you.' But her address is to all of us. Never was it truer to say: 'if you are not part of the solution you are part of the problem.'

Higher Education has a very particular role in questioning the content of our curriculum and the direction of our graduates. They ARE the solution. The creative industries can help lead the re-appraisal of how we live. At AUB we graduate students in a broad range of creative practice, all of which can lead the way in revisiting our expectations of life and the use of resources, biodiversity and climate change. **Why AUB Human?** Because we are the problem. We impact the non-human world more than any other influence on the planet. We disconnect from the consequences of our actions. **Why AUB Human?** Because our community of learning needs to raise our awareness of the ethics of practice and the consequences of our actions. Students need literacy in the new fundamentals: climate change, biodiversity and social justice.

In 2020 students of Architecture have actively engaged in broadening their awareness of the issues AUB Human helps to raise. Through their curriculum and integrated project work they consider the consequences of their designs, whether through understanding insulation, energy use, or the sustainability of their materials. The acknowledgement of AUB Human issues impacts many of our projects and especially the third-year final project, where issues of sustainability, biodiversity, biophilia, social justice, mindfulness, health and mental health are all explored by our students. These projects are not only encouraged but rewarded. We're proud that once again a BA Architecture graduate, Charley Harvey, was a winner of an AUB Sustainability Award. Another student, Deima Ambrazaitye, explored recycling throughout her third year, and concluded with a paper recycling facility built using timber and paper-based products. She even made her own paper. This imaginative use of paper won a John Purcell Paper Prize. A project on biophilia by Adam Primmer was a joint winner of the Terence and Annette O'Rourke Undergraduate Architecture Prize, shared with Charley Harvey.

AUB Human helps to create the wider 'ecology' of education in which to situate these course level actions. As students increasingly arrive with an awareness of their responsibilities to broaden their knowledge of human impact on the biosphere, AUB needs to continue to encourage and enhance their opportunities to learn about these issues and challenge establish norms.

Our graduates need to graduate equipped for a negative carbon world that rejects many of the accepted models of production developed in the previous two centuries of industrialisation, and create a new way of living between ourselves and our fellow human and non-human inhabitants.

Finally, the Corona-virus pandemic and our own campus shut down in March 2020 confronted us with the need to change. We can no longer separate economic, human and planetary health. Culturally we have had to re-evaluate what we value. Growth and wealth have been substituted by front-line health workers and life values. The coincident Black Lives Matter events have drawn our attention to issues of social equality and ethical practice. It is worth considering that seemingly innocent sculptures and public monuments have been a focus of protests. The 'new normal' has entered our language and engaged broader discussion than previously. We now accept that it is possible to radically change our way of life when we need to. We have done it to protect our own human health. Next we need to re-build the economy based on human, non-human and planetary health.

Never has AUB Human been more valuable to our learning community.

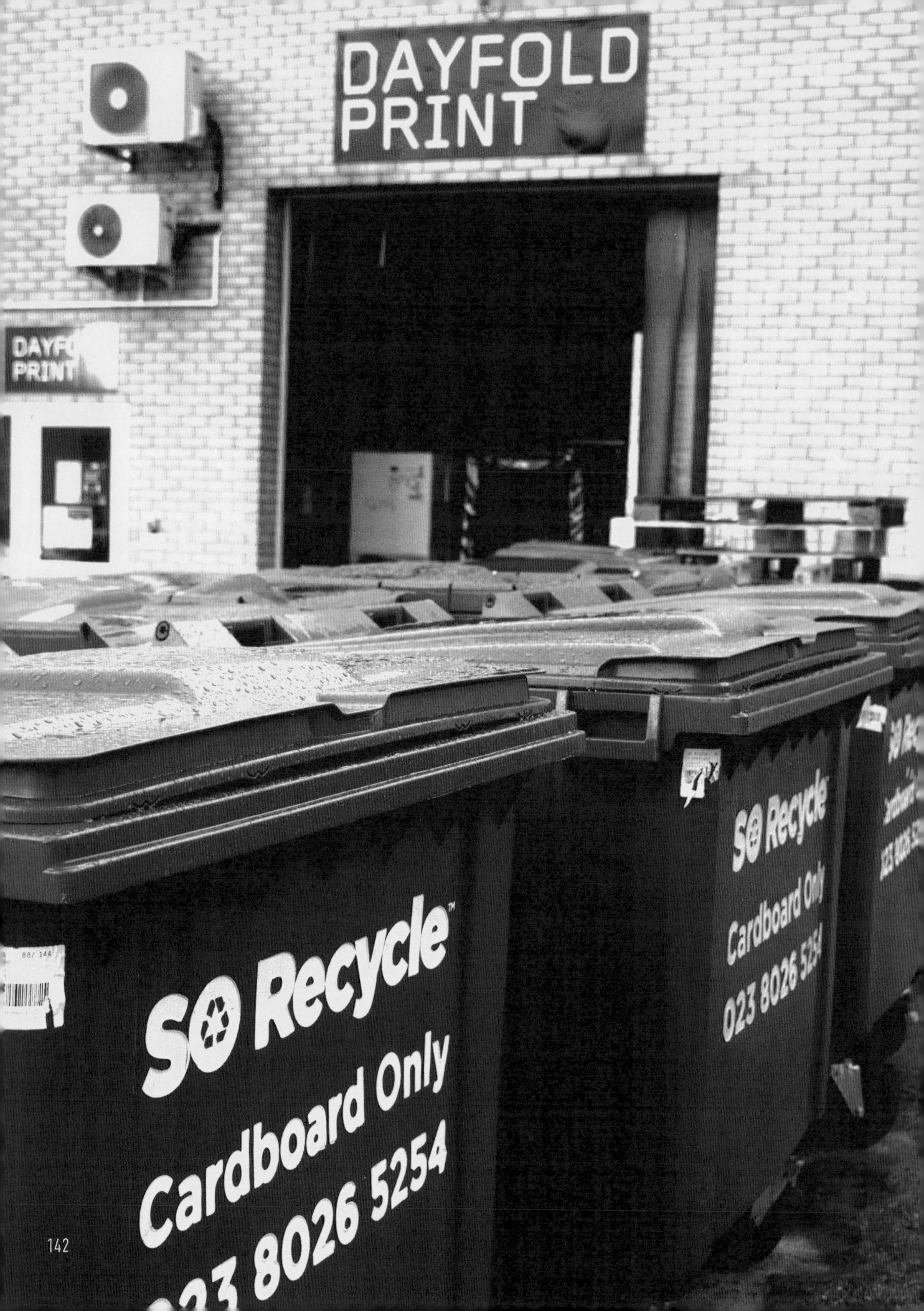
DAYFOLD
PRINT
SO Recycle
Cardboard Only
023 8026 5254

PRINTING THE BOOK

Natalie Carr, AUB Human intern

Ever since Alice and I started discussing how we would like to document the AUB Human events we had done this year, we knew we also wanted to make a printed book. This presented us with some deliberations as to whether AUB Human should actually be printing a book with all the associated environmental impacts of the process itself. We knew if we were going to make physical copies that we wanted it to have as little environmental impact as possible.

Printing ink is a minefield in itself, water-based inks and vegetable oil–based systems might have renewable source content, but you have to weigh up that sometimes these products actually use more energy in the drying process. We also considered using squid ink; it might be environmentally friendly but the process of extracting the ink from the squid didn't seem humane as the squid needs to be dead…a definite no.

In the end we visited our friends at Dayfold. They are an FSC certified printing company in Dorset and have printed many lovely publications for AUB. Dayfold have an ethos that aligns with ours when it comes to waste, recycling and their printing processes. They have two huge litho presses and a wonderful digital machine, all of which have their own pros and cons but each limit waste in their own way, from reducing water consumption to limiting ink wastage.

Finally we decided to print a small run using 'virgin' paper (paper from trees planted specifically for paper production). Dayfold advised us that the most sustainable paper they recommend is G. F. Smith Colourplan, a virgin paper created with an amount of recycled paper; each harvest requires planting more trees, resulting in an amount of carbon actually being removed from the footprint each time the paper is created. We also decided that I would be responsible for creating the laser cut covers which I would make here at AUB using our state of the art facilities.

We hope you enjoy reading it.

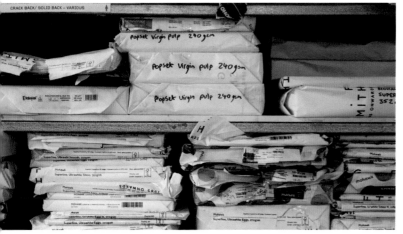

AUB HUMAN
RESEARCH GROUP

The AUB Human Research Group aims to foster a transdisciplinary community that explores 'creativity for good' through theoretical and practice-based research. When we consider the environmental, social and ethical global challenges that our world currently faces, it is our obligation as individuals, creatives and academics to be innovative and challenge current practice, systems and thinking in order that we can make a positive difference to the world. The AUB Human Research Group brings a critical and theoretical engagement to the intersection between these global challenges and the potential of creative solutions.

The AUB Human Research Group was founded by Alice Stevens in 2018. The research members have undertaken is broad ranging. This year Karen Ryan has been researching how sustainable fashion influencers can advocate for conscious consumption and mitigate the impact of fast fashion. Franziska Conrad and Lucy Devall have undertaken a research project in Zanzibar to develop maker manuals with the RNLI to help prevent drowning. Claire Holman's research explores how psychological safety can influence a positive culture and Monica Franchin and Alice Stevens have been undertaking research into salient imagery and how it can aid navigation for people with a cognitive impairment.

Please see the website for more information.

MEMBERS

Simon Beeson—Course Leader
BA (Hons) Architecture

James Cole—Course Leader,
BA (Hons) Creative Writing

Mark Collington—Senior Lecturer
BA (Hons) Animation

Fran Conrad—Course Leader
MA & BA (Hons) Design

Lucy Devall—Outreach Senior Officer
Innovation Studio

Anne Edwardes
BA (Hons) Photography

Ed Firth—Course Leader
Master of Architecture

Claire Flexen—Pathway Leader
Prep-HE

Monica Franchin—Senior Lecturer
BA (Hons) Interior Architecture

Claire Holman—Senior Lecturer
BA (Hons) Modelmaking

James Jackson
Sustainability, Estates

Sarah James—Senior Lecturer
BA (Hons) Visual Communication

Cathy John—Senior Lecturer
BA (Hons) Creative Events Management

Mark Osborne—Senior Lecturer
BA (Hons) Graphic Design

Hester Poole—Lecturer
Prep-HE

Rebecca Pride—Course Leader
BA (Hons) Costume and
Performance Design

JR Ryan
BA (Hons) Illustration

Karen Ryan—Senior Lecturer
BA (Hons) Fashion + BA (Hons) Fashion
Branding & Communication

Rebecca Savory Fuller—Senior Lecturer
BA (Hons) Acting

Alice Stevens—Senior Lecturer
BA (Hons) Graphic Design

Ed Ward—Lecturer,
BA (Hons) Interior Architecture

DOROTHY MACKENZIE

Chair of Governors

AUB Human is a pioneering initiative highlighting the potential for using creativity to effect positive change on the most urgent issues we face as a society, from the climate emergency to racial justice, over-consumption to mental and physical health. AUB Human asks challenging questions, encourages critical debate and inspires innovative solutions.

The events of 2020 have placed these issues at the heart of the future agenda for governments, businesses, education and communities, and the AUB Human approach has never felt more relevant and necessary. AUB as an institution, learning from the AUB Human experience, can weave this sense of responsibility and opportunity throughout its operations and academic practice. I am delighted to have been invited to join the Board of Governors of AUB at this challenging and exciting time and look forward to contributing to this.

I see AUB as an organisation that brings together a firm focus on the future with a skill base rich both in imaginative thinking and in practical, technical execution. As such, it will have a vital role to play as part of the creative industries and within the local economy and community, building new skills and finding innovative solutions that promote regeneration, restoration, wellbeing and equality.

Biography:
Dorothy Mackenzie is Co-Founder and Chair of the London operations of Dragon Rouge, a global creative agency. She's been active for many years in the drive to embed sustainability in design and business, from writing 'Green Design' in 1990, through her work with major brands to her involvement with organisations such as Green Alliance, Carbon Trust and the Ellen MacArthur Foundation.

AUB Human asks challenging questions, encourages critical debate and inspires innovative solutions

IMAGE CREDITS

Page 4: Speaker portraits. Supplied and used with kind permission of the subject. Pages 7, 10, 13, 15-17, 25-26, 27-28, 70-71, 73, 82-83,102: Alex Greatwich. 2019-20. Various. AUB. Page 22: Ram Shergill. 2016. Porcupine. Used with kind permission of the owner. Page 31, 32: Adele Keeley. 2019. Days for Girls, Gambia. Used with kind permission of the owner. Page 32: Jonathan Beal. 2019. Days for Girls. AUB. Page 34: Marten Sims. 2019. 21 Toys. AUB. Page 36-37: Mark Osborne. 2019. Empathy. AUB. Page 44: Paolo Rizzi. 2019. Portrait of Rosie Isbell. Used with kind permission of the owner via subject. Page 45: Speaker portraits. Supplied and used with kind permission of the subject. Page 47: T Levels Branding & Campaign. 2018. Used with kind permission of Philosophy via Tammy Johal. Page 51: Michael Pinksy. 2019. Pollution Pods On Brownsea Island. Used with kind permission of the owner. Page 52: Simon Beeson. 2019. Architecture Students. AUB. Page 54-55: Michael Pinksy. 2017. Enteringlondon-Tn. Used with kind permission of the owner. Page 58, 68: Bill Bradshaw. 2019. Brownsea Island. Used with kind permission of AUB marketing. Page 62-63: Ahmad Omar Aljabban. 2019. Pollution Pods. Used with kind permission of the owner. Page 64: Lucy Devall. 2019. Climate in Crisis. AUB. Page 70-71: Alex Greatwich. 2020. Fashion infographic by Ben Smitheman, Miranda Norman, Lucy Holland & Emily Butler. Audioscape by Martin Nachev, Eve Davie-Beaumont, Chloe Burridge. AUB. Page 78: AUBSU. 2019. Tree Planting Volunteer Day. Used with kind permission of AUBSU. Page 87: Gianluca Urdiroz Agati. 2019. A Letter from the Desert. Used with kind permission of Ana Clark Ribeiro. Page 94: Speaker portraits. Supplied and used with kind permission of the subject. Page 100: Paul Wenham-Clarke. 2019. The Urban Gypsies of The Westway. Used with kind permission of the owner. Page 108: Speaker portraits. Supplied and used with kind permission of the subject. Page 118: Anne Edwardes. 2018. Chrissy Levett. AUB. Page 127: Charley Harvey. 2020. The Urban Chine. Image courtesy of the owner. Pages 142, 144-147: Ed Hill. 2020. Dayfold. Used with kind permission of the owner.

BIBLIOGRAPHY

Human After All. (2020) Weapons Of Reason. [online]. Available at: https://weaponsofreason.com/about/ [Accessed 11.10.20]

Pinsky, M. (2020) Pollution Pods. [online]. Available at: http://www.michaelpinsky.com/project/pollution-pods/ [Accessed 03.10.20]

ACKNOWLEDGEMENTS

We would like to thank Emma Hunt and Marion Morrison for their ongoing encouragement and support of AUB Human, and the AUBSU for the opportunities they provide to students to engage with sustainability, ethical purchasing and consumption.

We would like to thank all the contributors, industry friends and alumni who share in the AUB Human philosophy and have given their time and support generously: Sevra Davis, Rebecca Ford, Ruth Andrade, Julian Thompson, Simon Widmer, Dorothy Mackenzie, Ram Shergill, Dr Sue Thomas, Rob Nicoll, Mark Chivers, Rosie Isbell, Izzi Hays, Tammy Johal, Olivia Gruitt, Kate Wood, Dom Kippin, Michael Pinsky, Martin Coyne, Paul Willoughby, Andrea Dell'Anna, Dayfold, Pali Palavathanan, Ted Hunt, Laura Yarrow, Paul Wenham-Clarke, Briony Hartley, Umesh Pandya, Chrissy Levett, Tom Tapper and Laura Jordan Bambach.

We would also like to thank our AUB colleagues for their valuable contributions to AUB Human over the past year, without whom the events would not have taken place: Prof. Paul Gough, Mark Osborne, Iain Archer, Karen Ryan, Dan Cox, Monica Franchin, Ed Ward, Dr. Christian McLening, Prof. Mary Oliver, Suzanna Hall, Christian Edwards, Louise Dennis, Simon Beeson, Poppy-Jay Palmer, Jonathan Beal, Adele Keeley, Rebecca Pride, Simon Pride, Nuala Clarke, Jon Reynard, Eden Frankham, Marten Sims, Lucy Duvall and James Jackson.

Finally, a thank you to all our students, a few of whom are featured in this book, who have risen to the challenges presented by the world today and used their creativity in showing how we can create a more sustainable and inclusive future for all: Isobel Fiske, Ahmad Omar Aljabban, Charley Harvey, Jordan Brew, Maisie Thomas, Eliza Reed, Katy Perks, Mia Cann, Natasha Fry, Ana Clark Ribeiro, Molly Board, Rania Qaddoura, Martin Nachev, Michael Rozen, Carl Doneza, Josh Papps, Katherine Weltch, Alexandra Csatari, Georgia Wilkins, Andy Burrow, Amelia Jackson, Racheal Conceicao, Ivaylo Nikolov, Luke Wadwell, Cynthia Porta Fernandez, Dominikus Kronwitter, Simona Dimitrova, Olivia Simpson, Katie Bridge, Sophie Corbin, Holly Gray, Logan Williams, Liam Marshall, Leon Newman, Brianna Barwell, Amelia Best, Tom Cornwell, Earthbourne, Ben Gage, Emily Duncan, Anna Freiesleben, Namrata Chandra, Sophie McPherson, Mary Hart, Stella Bonova, Neisha Rendel, Lotte Cassidy, Emma Rodak, Lucy Holland, Dan Trend, Ffion McCormack, Ben Smitheman, Miranda Norman, Emily Butler, Martin Nachev, Eve Davie-Beaumont, Ella Rose and Chloe Burridge.

BIOGRAPHIES

ALICE STEVENS

Alice is an RSA Fellow and Senior Lecturer in Graphic Design at Arts University Bournemouth. Her research focuses on social, ethical and sustainable design practice. Alice founded AUB Human in 2015 and has since curated various events and symposia that explore how creatives can make a positive difference to the lives of others, and use their skills as a force for global good.

NATALIE CARR

Natalie graduated from the BA (Hons) Graphic Design course at Arts University Bournemouth in 2018 and is the current AUB Human intern. Her interest in social, ethical and sustainable design solutions has enabled her to work with local businesses, CICs and the AUB Innovations team on beach-based community interventions within Bournemouth.

enables deeper
understanding
and an ability to
see problems
from another's
perspective
which is critical
to inclusive and
successful
design.

AUB HUMAN GAVE ME THE CONFIDENCE TO 'FAIL FAST'

Alongside this, I am
delighted to have
been accepted
onto Creative
Conscience's
Summer School,
which will take
the skills and
excitement to
design for change,
ignited in the AUB
Human events,
even further.

The tools enabled
me to literally
'walk in my user's
shoes' - I would
never have
experienced this
if it wasn't for
taking part in
the workshop.

...was a really nice
...ay of everyone
...ollaborating
...ogether.
...eople came
...university
...wing that they
...going to
a difference
...mebody.

As a museum we always enjoy
supporting AUB Human.
This year we looked at the theme
of New Narratives through
sustainable design in plastics
by exploring what makes a
product sustainable, how it can
be used to adapt and change
the uses of other things, and how
easily plastics objects can be
regenerated through recycling
or upcycling. MoDiP supports
teaching, learning, and research
across the AUB and beyond.

MODIP

New Narratives
in Plastics